D0002194

We are made to persist.
That's how we find out
who we are.

—Tobias Wolff, In Pharaoh's Army

Your Career Is an Extreme Sport

Eileen P. Gunn

▶▶ FOCUS ▶▶ DRIVE ▶▶ EXCEL ▶▶ ▶▶ ▶▶ ▶▶ ▶▶ ▶▶ ▶▶ ▶▶ ▶▶ ▶▶ ▶▶ ▶▶ ▶▶

adams
media

Hotchkiss Public Library
P.O. Box 540
Hotchkiss, CO 81419

Copyright © 2006 Quirk Packaging, Inc.
Text copyright © 2006 Eileen P. Gunn
Photographs pages 2–3 copyright © Ron Hilton; pages 14–15 copyright © Maciej Kawalski; pages 42–43 copyright © Mads Frederiksen; pages 68–69 copyright © Chris Zawada; pages 90–91 copyright © Paul Topp; pages 112–113 copyright © Bill Grove; pages 130–131 copyright © Jeff McDonald; pages 156–157 © Mads Frederiksen.

All rights reserved. This book, or parts thereof, may not be reproduced in any form without permission from the publisher; exceptions are made for brief excerpts used in published reviews.

Published by Adams Media, an F+W Publications Company
57 Littlefield Street
Avon, MA 02322
www.adamsmedia.com

 A Quirk Packaging Book
Edited by Sarah Scheffel
Designed by Stislow Design+Illustration

ISBN-10: 1-59337-611-1   ISBN-13: 978-1-59337-611-6

Printed in China

J I H G F E D C B A

Library of Congress Cataloging-in-Publication Data available from the publisher.

This publication is designed to provide accurate and authoritative information with regard to the subject matter covered. It is sold with the understanding that the publisher and packager are not engaged in rendering legal, accounting, or other professional advice. If legal advice or other expert assistance is required, the services of a competent professional person should be sought.
—From a *Declaration of Principles* jointly adopted by a Committee of the American Bar Association and a Committee of Publishers and Associations

Many of the designations used by manufacturers and sellers to distinguish their products are claimed as trademarks. Where those designations appear in this book and Adams Media was aware of a trademark claim, the designations have been printed in capital letters.

This book is available at quantity discounts for bulk purchases.
For information, please call 1-800-872-5627.

241659

			SHIP TO				
			ADDRESS				
			CITY, STATE, ZIP				
					HOW SHIP		DATE
NUMBER	DEPARTMENT	SALESPERSON	WHEN SHIP	TERMS	HOW SHIP		
						PRICE	AMOUNT

001

Introduction

THINK OF YOURSELF AS AN EXTREME ATHLETE AND YOUR CAREER AS THE ADVENTURE SPORT OF A LIFETIME.

Once upon a time, the typical career path was the equivalent of a ski run at a four-star resort. Sure, there might have been the occasional ice patch, and a few unexpected bumps or tight turns, but basically it would offer you a well-groomed and predictable course from beginning to end. You could expect lifetime employment, and a clear and obvious career trajectory. At the end of a good run, your loyalty would be rewarded with a comfortable pension, lifetime health insurance, and that proverbial gold watch.

This path offered you comfort, security, and a reliable social contract. It was nice. But it could be limiting. If that particular hill didn't suit your personal style or interests, you didn't have many other options—all the other runs were pretty much the same.

In contrast, today's work landscape seems to offer nothing but moguls and ruts, steep trajectories and unmarked trails—the equivalent of freestyle or off-trail skiing.

Consider: Job tenure today is typically only four to six years, and it gets shorter with each new generation that enters the workforce. A person can easily have seven to ten jobs, or more, over the course of his or her professional life—and as many employers.

And, as if all those transitions aren't tricky enough to navigate, chances are good they won't all be voluntary. In 2004, some 93 percent of Americans who lost their jobs were laid off, the result of corporate downsizing, mergers, or reorganizations.

What's really scary? The rate of layoffs has actually been going up as the economy has been getting better. Recent research shows the portion of job losses that were layoffs rose sharply from 64 percent in 2001, the year the bottom last fell out of the U.S. economy, to 75 percent in 2002, and 79 percent in 2003. DBM, the outplacement-counseling firm that did the study, expects the trend to continue. Layoffs, once symptoms of ailing industries or slow economies, have become business-as-usual, as large companies continually reorganize and reshuffle to keep themselves agile and dynamic (or at least looking that way).

But what's really sobering is that the professionals who have managed to remain employed and on some kind of certifiable career path through all these twists and turns aren't necessarily happy. They don't see themselves as the lucky ones.

The consulting giant Accenture surveyed middle managers in 2005, and found that more than half did not respect the organizations they worked for; exactly one-third thought their companies were flat-out mismanaged.

Today's work landscape seems to offer nothing but moguls and ruts, steep trajectories and unmarked trails.

The main source of their misery was how their companies treated them as individuals. Some 38 percent thought they did way more work than they got credit for (flat pay and scarce promotions might have something to do with that). And 35 percent couldn't see a clear career path for themselves.

Among the broader workforce, dissatisfaction is even more rampant. The consulting firm Towers Perrin surveyed 85,000 people who work for large or midsize companies and found that only 14 percent feel engaged in their jobs and are willing to go the extra mile for their employers. Again, it comes down to

Rather than waiting for employers to figure things out and lead the way, it's time to get extreme and change the way *you* think about your job and your career.

how the companies treat their employees, and their failure to create an environment conducive to working well. Fifty-nine percent of these workers don't see their bosses supporting new ideas or new ways of doing things, and 60 percent doubt their companies' values are consistent with their own.

If you're just entering the workforce or still relatively new in your career, these statistics might make you want to quit your job and move back into your parents' basement. But companies can't bear all the blame for this chronic dissatisfaction.

We've known for at least twenty years that the way employers think about work and their workforce has changed, but the way they approach employee relations and career development hasn't kept pace. They expect the same things they always have from their staff, but too many either don't know how to replace the old-style rewards of lifetime employment and a reliably comfortable retirement or haven't tried—they just come up short. Consider: Your dad worked hard and had his stress, but most likely he was almost always home for dinner and around on the weekends. His attention at your little league game or dance recital was never diverted by a persistent cell phone or BlackBerry. He got regular raises and his company was storing up a real pension for him. In sum, his job and his career were one and the same.

In contrast, long hours are now de rigueur, but raises and regular promotions aren't. No matter how far from the office you might roam, you're still tethered to it by e-mail and cell phone—until they cut you loose in a layoff that probably has more to do with the company's latest strategic shift than its financial health. You get to save for your own retirement with a 401(k), which should provide for your later years, if you actually put as much as you're supposed to into it and invest well—and don't pour everything blindly into your company's stock the way so many Enron and Worldcom employees did.

Rather than waiting for employers to figure things out and lead the way, it's time to get extreme and change the way *you* think about your job and your career, which today are distinct and separate things.

Those of us who are steering ourselves through this fractured landscape have a choice: We can let ourselves be psyched out, and watch our careers stall as one obstacle after another trips us up, or we can embrace the risks and opportunities presented by this unrestricted and uncharted terrain. We can get results from these challenges that our parents and grandparents didn't even dream about and carve out career paths that really suit us.

To do that, we need new role models and a new vocabulary to talk about our work and careers.

Americans, the sports nuts that we are, spent most of the last century talking about work using the language of baseball and football—that century's iconic team sports. But those metaphors no longer fit. How worthwhile is it to be a "dedicated team player" when managers are totally fickle about who they keep in the game, who they bench, and who they trade? If we're unlikely to get all the way to the end of the season, or even the bottom of the ninth with the rest of the starters, why devote ourselves to racking up points for the home team? Batting in someone else's run might not win you the attention or financial reward it once would have, so why not instead think in terms of grabbing big air off a steep drop-off, landing a 720-degree jump in the half-pipe, or coming out the far side of class-5 rapids—whatever solo feat is going to catch people's attention, prove your abilities, and give you a thrill, regardless of how you wind up plying your trade or for whom.

Sure, day-to-day work is still about teamwork, but your career is absolutely a solo endeavor. As you migrate from one job, company, or type of work to another, perhaps many times over in the course of your lifetime, the one thing that remains constant is *you*—the work that turns you on, the skills you think are cool, and goals you set for your life's work. You alone are responsible for making sure you stay focused on those things and find ways to nail them.

So, what are the sports that show us how to succeed as individuals and score points for ourselves? Extreme sports, which are gearing up to be the iconic sports of the 21st century. Think motocross and mountain biking, snowboarding and sky-diving, adventure racing and surfing, to name just a handful.

If you're anything like your Generations X and Y peers, at least one of these activities is capturing your imagination and possibly a great deal of your leisure time, too. Young, upwardly mobile types are trading in skis for snowboards, golf clubs for mountain bikes, and tennis rackets for carabiners and rope. They do triathlons and run marathons. They spend their vacations trekking in the Andes, kayaking the Rogue River, and surfing in Maui. (Sound like anyone you know? Sound like you?)

They're bringing what they learn at play back to the office, where, to build a satisfying career, you need to be self-reliant and self-confident, and have a high risk-tolerance. To summit a peak or surf a big wave, you have to have awesome athletic skills—and in the workplace, you have to have awesome skills that you can count on when it matters, too. Extreme sports give us the perfect framework for talking about and realizing success in the new, extreme business environment.

Those middle managers, disgruntled because their bosses haven't laid out a clear career path for them, aren't necessarily being neglected. But they're missing an opportunity by waiting for someone else to take care of something they should be taking care of themselves. If extreme athletes are strong individuals who seize opportunities and take their lives into their own hands, then extreme careerists are strong individuals who take charge of their own destinies in the workplace instead of waiting around for their employers to create their success. (They won't.)

Think of it this way: A career is no longer a linear path that some paternal authority lays out for you; it's a portfolio of projects and assignments and jobs. It's up to you to decide what work will go into your collection and what shape your career takes over time. Sure, it takes more thought and energy to build a career this way, but it's also more satisfying than letting someone else shape your future to suit their needs.

Similarly, those workers who believe their employers don't share their values aren't necessarily working for bad companies. But they're each working for the wrong company for them. Organizations big and small have their own personalities, cultures, and values. So, like extreme athletes, workers today need to be aggressive and take control of their situations. No more lifetime employment? So what. Work that job mobility to your advantage by being on the lookout for new opportunities and by holding out for a workplace that really suits you. Whether you're interviewing for your first job or you're further along on your career path, making choices that allow you to maintain your individuality—rather than tying your identity to your employer—is essential today.

More and more people are already doing it.

Extreme careerists are strong individuals who take charge of their own destinies in the workplace instead of waiting around for their employers to create their success.

The Families and Work Institute estimates that one in five people in America works for themselves. Thirty percent of these people are small-business owners with employees. They tend to work longer hours and earn more than the average person, which is something they value. The rest are solo practitioners who left traditional jobs at least partly because they value their work-life balance. They tend to work fewer hours than most people, and enjoy greater freedom to define where and when and with whom they work.

It's not a matter of choosing whether or not to take on risk; it's a matter of deciding what kind of risk you're willing to take and what you stand to gain from it.

The self-employed are more likely than those who work for others to observe that their jobs require creativity and that they're developing the skills and abilities they aspire to attain.

This isn't to say that you have to be your own boss to be happy, but it does demonstrate that people who are true to who they are, who think about what they want and what they value and how they want to work—and who take advantage of the new business environment to make it happen—are more satisfied than those who wait for Papa Corporation to take care of them.

Sound risky? Absolutely. Extreme athletes understand that you can't run away from risk if you want to excel at something challenging. But you don't have to abandon yourself to it either.

Some thirty years ago, psychologist Bruce Ogilvie tested athletes who excelled at a variety of extreme sports, like skydiving and racecar driving, and found that they possessed above-average intelligence, emotional stability, and independence. Contrary to the stereotype of extreme athletes as daredevils with a death wish, it was also discovered that they made concerted efforts to minimize the dangers they exposed themselves to.

Like these athletes, you need to accept that risk plays a role in your career and understand how to balance it with opportunity.

Embracing an extreme career means making the new work environment work for you. For example, if you understand that you have no guarantee of lifetime employment and should expect routine layoffs, then as long as you work for someone else, you live with the risk of losing your job every day. That should make the option of leaving a job to try something new or going out on your own less daunting. It's not a matter of choosing whether or not to take on risk; it's a matter of deciding what kind of risk you're willing to take and what you stand to gain from it.

In addition, knowing you are likely to have seven to ten different jobs in your lifetime makes it seem a little less risky to try something new and challenging now. After all, if a venture doesn't work out, at worst you're out of just one job. You can pick yourself up, learn what you can from the experience, and move on to the next thing (which you would eventually do anyway). You aren't forfeiting your life's work, as would have been the case for an earlier generation.

Your Career Is an Extreme Sport invites you to think of yourself as an extreme athlete and your career as the adventure sport of a lifetime. It will help you to get stoked about what you do, embrace risk, go for big air, lead with skill, stand out with confidence, and embrace the obstacle course that is today's business world.

This book won't provide a map to the course (there isn't a map, or a fixed course for that matter); instead it will teach you how to think your way through it. In short, it will show you how to treat your career like the extreme sport that it is, so you can pursue your work with aggression, skill, style, and grace—and always land on your feet.

Are you ready?

Navigational Tools

These symbols will help you chart your course through this book.

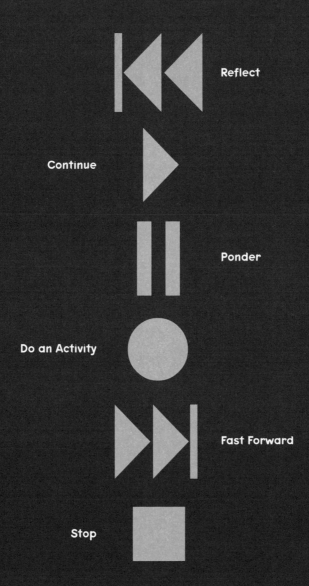

Reflect

Continue

Ponder

Do an Activity

Fast Forward

Stop

If you want an extreme career, you have to embrace risk as part of your reality every day. ▷

FAX (

Chapter 1
Are You Ready to Get on the Extreme Track?

WHAT *IS* AN EXTREME CAREER? READ ON. ▸ Stacy Peralta became a pro skateboarder in the 1970s, at a time when such a role didn't really exist—at least not in the way we think of it today. There was no EXPN, no X Games, no high-tech video games, and no one promoting action sports to sell everything from soda to clothing

He made it up as he went along, figuring out just how far he could take both his career and skateboarding in general. He parlayed championship wins into media attention, sponsorship deals, and an ownership stake in Powell-Peralta, a skateboard company that made millions and sponsored Tony Hawk, the most successful skateboarder in the world today, before he became a household name.

In an article that Peralta wrote for a skateboarding magazine, he described the ultimate skater as someone who has "awesome aggression and style, power and fury, wild abandon, destruction of all fear, untamed individualism, and a free-spirited determination to tear, shred, and rip relentlessly."

Man!

It's mind-blowing to contemplate what would happen if you could apply that attitude to your life and work. But if you adopted that powerful full-on persona and walked into your cube farm with it, no doubt you'd scare your officemates.

So, what does it mean to treat your career as an extreme sport?

First things first: **You need to destroy fear.**

Why? To accomplish anything in life, much less anything of significance, you have to expose yourself. You have to put something on the line. You have to accept risk as part of your reality.

Right now, you might want to get a promotion or pursue a new job with more responsibility than you've ever had. Or maybe you have an idea for an entirely new product or service you think your company should offer. You might be itching to go out on your first solo sales call, or take the lead on a major case or project or presentation. Or you might believe the time is right to start your own practice or business. These are the sorts of risks you'll take again and again in order to grow your career—in big and small ways.

But each time you try something new, you'll have to step out of your comfort zone and face the possibility of screwing up, or even falling flat on your face. And the higher you climb in your career, the larger the risk. You might simply be embarrassed; you might make some mistakes or wind up forfeiting some of that hard-won respect. Let's face it, you might lose your job or your business or even your life savings.

But the flip side of embracing risk is the chance to fully realize your individuality. Confront your fears head on and you'll discover your own ability to "tear, shred, and rip relentlessly." The reward is that you get to be true to yourself in your work and in your life.

Whether you are in finance or law or advertising or media or technology or consulting or biotechnology, you probably don't yet know the limits of your abilities and skills. Wouldn't finding out be a trip?

Like Peralta looking at the skating scene in the mid-70s, you probably suspect that the boundaries of your profession or business are not where other people think they are or want them to be; they're just a little further out.

Even extreme athletes like Peralta and Hawk, big-wave surfer Laird Hamilton, and Olympic gold-medal snowboarder Kelly Clark might never find the absolute brick-wall end of their capabilities. But that's not really the point. By getting out and practicing every day, and by pushing themselves further and further, they become better athletes than those who came before them—and maybe better than even they thought they could be. Then they put those mad skills on display by winning competitions, and that success allows

them to create even bigger opportunities for themselves, such as sponsors to pay for their gear and travel. It also opens up possibilities that they might not have been looking for but that are huge nonetheless—like the chance to design snowboards or video games or launch their own companies.

And aside from everything else, these extreme athletes think it's fun to just get out there and do what they do every day.

Your career can be just like that.

The flip side of embracing risk is the chance to fully realize your individuality. The reward is that you get to be true to yourself in your work and in your life.

destroy

fear.

Consider **Rick Alden,** a serial entrepreneur now in his early forties who started his first company, which organized and promoted pro and amateur snowboard events, while he was an undergrad marketing major at the University of Colorado. He sold it when he was in his late twenties. Later, he set out to design a new boot-and-binding system for snowboards. He launched Device Boots & Bindings, and three years later sold that.

He's now on his third company, called Skullcandy. This one makes durable headphones, and also helmets and backpacks with speakers built in, so you can listen to your MP3 player when you're out snowboarding or skiing or skating.

On his resume, he says that as the founder and CEO of Skullcandy, he's responsible for the "design, development, and distribution of mind-blowing, punk rock consumer electronic products." Alden has fashioned a career for himself built on a kick-ass independent attitude. He's done so by dreaming up products he thinks are cool and assuming that if he digs his ideas, other snowboarders will, too. Then he plunges ahead and devotes himself to seeing whether he can make and sell them successfully. He sees this focus on individuality and self-determination as a completely organic outgrowth of the snowboarding he's been doing for most of his life.

"In snowboarding, I can do whatever I want. If I see a huge embankment, I can cut hard and go up the side of it and totally rip it up, and then go find another one. I can ride as fast as I want and as hard as I want—and [not] damage anything," he says. "Coming up with an idea for a new product is like seeing a bank on the side of my business. We'll rip it up. We'll play around with it a little. And if it doesn't work we won't do it, but it was fun to try."

You'll have your own vision of what it means to tear through an awesome snow bank. It could be a level of responsibility you're seeking, or a person or company you're dying to work with, or a way of working, a product you're itching to develop, or a magical sum of money you're determined to earn.

Where to start?

x

---

tear, shred,
rip relentlessly

You'll do your best to "tear, shred, and rip relentlessly" at your work every day. 023 Whether your field is web design or journalism or product development or marketing or law or financial analysis, you'll work on your skills and push your edge. That includes bringing new ideas to meetings, developing proposals to present to your boss's boss, volunteering to solo on a project or run a meeting, or taking charge of a hairy situation no one else wants to manage. Even when the risks you face fill you with fear, you'll bring it on.

And if you execute your skills with style and "awesome aggression" (which is just another way of saying *confidence*), you can create the opportunities you want. Prospects you might not have been looking for but that are cool will present themselves, too (maybe in the form of a call from a headhunter or someone from a rival company inviting you to lunch).

Layer these opportunities one on top of the other, and over time you will have more than a job and more than a specialty; you will have what can accurately be described as an extreme career. The fact that no one has laid out a career path for you will be irrelevant because you'll have chosen a line for yourself and dropped in with everything you've got.

A few words of caution:

▌▌ If you aren't stoked about your job, do some soul-searching—and maybe some job-hopping—before you set yourself on an extreme course. No matter what you do and how much money you make, your work is too large a part of your life to feel anything less than passionate about it.

▌▌ If you're still a freshman in your field, consider coasting the beginner slopes for a little while. Most people need a few years of accumulated knowledge and experience behind them before they are ready to set their own big goals and perform the truly radical maneuvers that will get them closer to achieving them.

▌▌ If you've paid your dues—maybe changed careers once or twice, finished grad school, survived your company's training program, or been promoted beyond your grunt-work, bottom-rung job to a post where you have real responsibility and the chance to stand out—then you're ready to rev up your career to an extreme level.

▸ Spend enough time talking to people who think activities like backcountry snowboarding, big-wave surfing, rock climbing, skydiving, adventure racing, motocross, long-distance biking, or transoceanic sailing are a big fun, and you might be surprised by what they actually say.

Strength, agility, speed, and physical stamina come up, of course, but only in passing—because they're a given. The skills and characteristics these extreme athletes *really* value and nurture have much more to do with their brains than their brawn, and are harder to come by.

Take, for example, free skiing. If you want to try this extreme sport, forget about manicured trails. Forget about thinking you rock because you can dig your edges in hard and hang on all the way down to the bottom of a little ol' double black diamond in fresh powder.

The skills and characteristics these extreme athletes really value and nurture have much more to do with their brains than their brawn.

A free-skiing run offers up deep snow, tight turns, stomach-churning drop-offs, fifty-five-degree slopes, bushes, and boulders—all right in your path. There are stretches that are designated no-fall zones because if you go right when you ought to dig hard to the left, or you slow down when you need speed, you'll fall. And if you fall, you will break your skis, maybe your poles, and probably your bones as you ragdoll downhill for forty or fifty feet.

It's no bunny slope.

Each skier navigates his or her path to the bottom and is judged by how tough a route they take, and by their aggressiveness, control, fluidity, and technique. "It's a full-on adrenaline rush before you drop in, just standing in the gate," says Trey Gregory, a thirty-something public relations executive who spent a year competing on the free-ski circuit, sponsored by the ski-gear company Atomic.

How do you get to the bottom of a free-ski run in winning form (or at least in one piece)?

You find out as much as you can about the run beforehand. You might take photographs from the bottom of the hill so you can choose a route and think about how to attack it. Once you're up top, you fully commit to the idea that this treacherous course *can* be skied and that *you* can ski it. Then you swallow your fear, launch yourself, and apply every ounce of mental agility and skill you have to analyzing and reacting on the fly.

You also have to be honest with yourself about your limits and abilities on any particular day and run. Ski a line beyond your skill level because you think *that* will impress the judges, and you will no doubt wind up doing your best impression of Wile E. Coyote as his ACME rocket skis carry him off a cliff and into thin air, where he whips out his little sign that reads, **YIKES!**

027

Benjamin Wagner, *an ambitious thirty-something, is one of two executive producers at MTV News—he manages the online side of the operation and is a six-time veteran of the New York City Marathon. He wrote this in his blog after his fifth run:*

028 I'll never really know what sustains me through the bone-crushing pain of the marathon. There's no real reason for doing it except that, for me, it is so f'ing difficult, it is so beyond explanation, that the mere completion of it is enough to remind me that, though life will continue to throw seemingly insurmountable and incomprehensible challenges my way, I will persist.

One such insurmountable challenge pops up once a year at work in the form of the MTV Video Music Awards. "We spend months planning," he says.

The 2005 awards were a particular feat of endurance and creative management because it was the first year Wagner had to present a full menu of live and packaged coverage for both MTVNews.com and a separate broadband website where fans could stream video.

Wagner recalls, "We had morning, noon, and night coverage of all the hoopla around the event—a week of concerts and parties; sometimes news happens (in 2005, Hurricane Katrina rolled ashore in Miami, where the awards were held, that night). I had a dozen photographers on standby, including shooters just for the broadband. We covered three dozen events, talked to people, did red carpet fashion photography, and featured the cars and boats people arrived in."

His group had to keep pace, minute by minute, with the live televised coverage of the awards and the after-party. And they couldn't do it from MTV's cushy, tech-laden offices above Times Square in New York but from an impromptu operating center in Miami.

In short, he says, "We had to have ten times the content we normally have, from a building with no infrastructure, in a medium we'd never tested that way." Under normal circumstances, it's not unusual for him to get by on very little sleep over the days leading up to the show.

It's the kind of extreme situation where you know not everything will go smoothly. "You hope it's things like the wrong computers showing up or not having enough RAM or your bandwidth choking because those problems are easy—you can throw money at them," he jokes.

The tougher problems come from "keeping people motivated and excited when they've been pushing for four days and have barely slept and are starting to flag. You have to make sure they still meet the deadlines, and make sure that what they do rocks." That's where having the psychological stamina and endurance to run for four hours straight becomes valuable. The belief that just because something seems impossible doesn't mean you can't work your way through it is "what has them lined up at my door," he says.

The marathoner explains, "I'm not the storm in the storm. I've been in situations where there was chaos going on around me and I was smiling. Someone would ask, 'What are you smiling about?' The person who asked was freaking out. But I was smiling because I knew I had it under control." His aim, besides demonstrating his skill and his style to those above him, is to create an environment that works for the people working below him. "I hope that I'm considered approachable and that someone can come to me and say, 'I don't know what to do here.'"

In a way, the VMAs are just another marathon, and Wagner manages them in the same way, by breaking down problems and tackling them mile by mile, obstacle by obstacle, until he gets to the finish.

029

SINGLE-MINDED
FOCUS

PSYCHOLOGICAL
STAMINA

ANALYTICAL
PROWESS

RISK TOLERANCE

INDIVIDUALITY

CRUCIAL CHARACTERISTICS OF WINNERS. ▸ These are the qualities that extreme athletes value because they are the qualities that separate the winners from the runners-up. So, how do they relate to your work world? Take a look.

SINGLE-MINDED FOCUS

What is it? The ability to single out an immediate goal and then pour your entire physical, mental, and emotional being into reaching it.

What does it look like? The opposite of multitasking. Decide what you *really* need to be doing now, devote your full attention to it, do it well, and move on.

When do you need it most? When you don't have nearly as much time as you think you need to finish a project, and you know you need to not only get it done but impress the hell out of everyone around you, from a big boss to a big client.

How can it go wrong? It turns into tunnel vision. You reject suggestions or feedback from coworkers because you're afraid they'll take too long or take you off course.   031

PSYCHOLOGICAL STAMINA

What is it? The ability to retain your integrity, purpose, and focus through long hours and myriad difficulties.

What does it look like? When everything is going wrong and everyone around you is demoralized, frazzled, and biting each other's heads off, psychological stamina allows you to block out the chaos, stay calm, and figure out how to get things back on track.

When do you need it? When you are working through a huge, complex, long-term project where things are without a doubt going to stray off course.

How can it go wrong? If you brush aside the fact that there is a problem, or downplay it instead of acknowledging and managing it, your coworkers will think you lack empathy, resent you, and be reluctant to pull together as a team.

ANALYTICAL PROWESS

What is it? The ability to break down a complex problem into bite-size pieces and methodically work through them.

What does it look like? Business as usual in a research lab.

When do you need it? When a task or problem is so complex that trying to absorb it all at once makes your brain hurt.

How can it go wrong? Problems become way more interesting than people. Coworkers stop inviting you to lunch or meetings or onto project teams because you've lost the ability to hold a casual conversation and aren't very interesting or social.

RISK TOLERANCE

What is it? We've already introduced the importance of risk, but, simply put, you need the ability to understand and accept risk and manage your way through it.

What does it look like? You present a daring idea at a meeting with the toughest boss in your department—and get it approved—because you spent hours discreetly doing research and practicing your pitch to make sure it would blow everyone away.

When do you need it? Anytime you want to do anything that's a departure from your actual job description.

How can it go wrong? You embrace risk so much, you believe it always has to be there, and you expose yourself and your team to it when a simpler, safer course is actually the smarter choice.

What is it? The strength and honesty to know who you are and the confidence to be that person consistently.

What does it look like? You strive to shape your work and your career path according to your personal goals and interests.

When do you need it? Anytime you make a decision about your work or your career.

How can it go wrong? You're not so much centered as self-centered. You blow off good advice and discount how your decisions affect others, alienating would-be supporters.

So, what about *you*?

Being on the corporate fast track, running your own fast-growth company, or making your own hours, while also making a pile of money as a free agent, can be as ripping and adrenaline-pumping as anything any free-style course can throw at you.

Making the big sale, bringing in the coveted client, meeting the killer deadline, or sealing the deal that secures crucial funding can bring on the same rush a snowboarder gets when she nails a new trick.

Just ask Rick Alden:

"I remember going to a ski hill once and seeing a guy using my boots and bindings. And it wasn't someone I knew....I realized this guy went to a retailer and picked my bindings out from over thirty others and ripped out hard cash to pay for them. I never had a bigger high in my life."

See if you've got what it takes to rip and shred your way through your work life.

033

1. You're planning your next vacation. You're ideal spot is:

❑ A. The same bungalow your family has been visiting since you were five.

❑ B. Someplace you've never been (and, ideally, have only recently heard of).

❑ C. Someplace on the State Department's travel-advisory list—those warnings are always overblown.

2. Your team was just assigned a cool new project. You:

❑ A. Support your boss's idea, as usual.

❑ B. Lobby for the most promising idea proposed by one of your team members, even though it's untested.

❑ C. Shamelessly promote your own idea.

034

3. When you settle on something you want—a cool job, a car that's a little out of your price range, a new sport that you'd like to master—you:

❑ A. Keep it in the back of your mind, but don't change your day-to-day routine.

❑ B. Figure out what you need to do to make it happen, set a deadline, and start working toward it.

❑ C. Go for it—life's too short for caution.

4. Your boss tells you a project has just been drastically revised and the team is going to have to work late...again. You:

❑ A. Resign yourself to a long night and feel stressed just thinking about it—you reach for the bag of Cheetos in your desk and start scarfing.

❑ B. Take a time-out to renew your focus, grab a Clif Bar, and start chipping away at the problem—the sooner it's resolved, the sooner everyone goes home.

❑ C. Think "Woo-hoo! Overtime! Line up the Jolt Colas!"

5. You're offered a job that's exciting but definitely beyond your skill level. You:

    ❑ A. Turn it down! Something else will come along when you feel more ready.

    ❑ B. Take it but start working on the skills you think you're short on so you can make a killer first impression.

    ❑ C. Take it and dive in: What could go wrong?

If you picked mostly As: The only thing extreme about you is your complacency. You don't naturally ooze determination, individuality, aggressiveness, or risk tolerance. So, take a long, hard look at yourself, where you are, and where you want to be.

Part of growing and succeeding is pushing yourself out of your comfort zone and working on the things you know you're kinda lame at. Can you swallow your fear and cultivate some of those characteristics in yourself? Will that be enough to get you where you want to go? And is it worth what it might take out of you?

If not, recalibrate your expectations and trade in your unused surfboard for a whistle—peewee soccer and that shiny lawnmower are waiting for you.

035

If you picked mostly Cs: I hope you're wearing a helmet and elbow pads, dude. There's a difference between gutsy and reckless, and you're in the kamikaze zone.

People can push their way to success through extreme aggression, reckless-ness, and doggedness, but it's fleeting and usually ends in a skull-shattering face plant. (Think Enron's Jeffrey Skilling, junk-bond bad boy Michael Milken, disgraced *New York Times* reporter Jayson Blair, or Nick Leeson, who destroyed Barings Bank by racking up more than one billion dollars in bad trades.) If you don't prepare or think your way through situations or separate good risks from bad ones, sooner or later you're gonna hit a rock and wipe out. Moreover, people shun those who are blatantly self-serving, so don't expect others to rally around you when you fall—your coworkers will be too busy smirking at each other to assist you.

If you picked mostly Bs: You're willing to stand out from the crowd and take calculated risks, and you do it in a way that makes people want to follow you. You also have the mental stamina, focus, and commitment you need to meet the tough goals you set for yourself. Rev yourself up for your extreme career (cue the high-volume alt-rock soundtrack).

Expand Your Comfort Zone

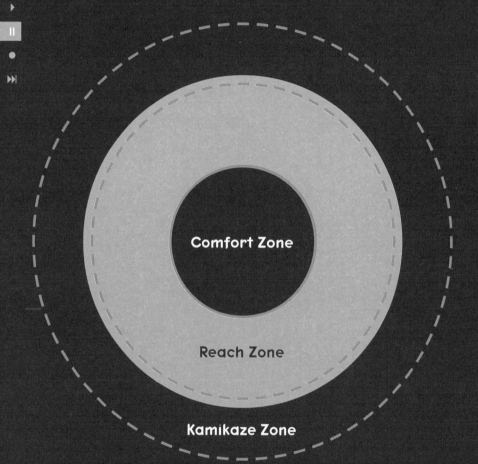

Comfort Zone

Reach Zone

Kamikaze Zone

REACH ZONE =

THE PLACE WHERE REAL GROWTH CAN HAPPEN

Torin Pavia *is the CEO of Arbitech, a $150 million business that buys and sells computer equipment the way Wall Streeters trade stocks and bonds. From a Southern California trading floor, a team of Tums-popping salespeople works at lightning speed to find the latest equipment at the lowest prices for their customers. They take orders from corporations and fill them in minutes by chasing down known sources, or they might come across a cache of inventory at a great price and go long—buying it in hopes of placing it later.*

Pavia says he's fired only two people in more than ten years as an entrepreneur. One of them was a kamikaze salesman who probably would have picked a lot of Cs in our extreme quiz.

When Pavia was running his first company just a few years out of college, an organic grocery store and café in Southern California, a group of guys barely old enough to drink pulled up almost daily for lunch. They drove Ferraris, competed in motocross races, and sold memory chips. They'd skipped college but were clearly working short hours, making far more money—and getting a far bigger rush—than Pavia was during his seventy-hour workweeks selling apples and vitamins.

So, after a few years, Pavia sold out to his partner and began looking for something where the profit-to-time ratio was better. He earned a living selling computer memory, and then on the trading desks of a series of small brokers while going to business school. Eventually, he and a B-school buddy took their classroom theories and trading-desk know-how and launched Arbitech. In need of tech-savvy salespeople who could handle the fast-paced trading he had in mind, he tracked down those motocross riders and hired a bunch of them.

But he quickly learned that putting adrenaline junkies on a high-speed trading floor is like letting a sugar addict lose in a candy factory.

One of these guys "loved risk" way too much. "If the order didn't have a high risk, he wouldn't take it," Pavia recalls. But his jump-first-and-make-it-work-later tactics scared away customers. And more than once he stuck Arbitech with inventory that was cheap enough but just wasn't in demand.

"He was so good at making people's minds up for them, he took on too much risk up front," says Pavia, "How does someone like that perform when it's no longer quick, easy money they're chasing? How do they keep their work ethic?"

They don't. Tired of cleaning up his messes, Pavia traded in this guy and his motocross buddies for a sales team that could balance instinct and intellect. He sought out adrenaline-deprived MBAs, attorneys, and corporate refugees who took to Arbitech's high-speed, high-risk pace—and had their own extreme hobbies, like surfing.

What was the difference between the new sales team and their predecessor? **039** They understood that there was risk in the work they were doing, and were comfortable with it. But they didn't love risk for the sake of risk, and knew that it wasn't an end but a means. They had a healthy respect for the downside and didn't expose themselves to it unnecessarily.

The result: They analyzed situations and chose their waves rather than diving blindly into anything that looked like deep water.

And Arbitech has been growing like nobody's business ever since.

PAST ONE

At some point you just have to go for big air and trust that the focus, skills, and instincts you've been cultivating will give you what you need.

040

SO, YOU KNOW YOU'RE IN THE ZONE. NOW WHAT? ▸ You have the inclination and you're actively cultivating the extreme characteristics—the focus, psychological stamina, analytical prowess, risk tolerance, and, yes, the individuality to kick some serious ass—that'll prove crucial to your success.

But understand that there's really no way to practice dropping out of a helicopter to ski Mont Blanc or pedaling across Moab in an endurance bike race. For athletes, these bigger challenges are the unmapped terrain. When the time comes to perform the next feat, it's going to be way different from the last mountain they skied or any other course they've raced.

Similarly, in the business world, there's no way to practice being put in charge of a huge budget or major project or an entire team. There's no test run when it comes to starting a business from the ground up or going out on your own to work as a free agent.

At some point, you just have to throw down what you've got and trust that the focus, skills, and instincts you've been cultivating will give you what you need to recognize the dangerous banks and sudden turns, and to be able to react on a dime and keep going.

Of course, if you jump from that helicopter before you've even mastered advanced skiing techniques on a traditional course, you'll flip and fall and break your bones while showing yourself to be the amateur you are.

It happened to free skier Trey Gregory. In his very first competition he pulled a tougher line than he really knew how to handle, and on his first big drop he landed badly. He lost one of his skis, couldn't finish the run, "and scored a big fat goose egg." He spent the rest of the season picking his routes more realistically—and finishing his runs well enough to actually score and place.

You want to feel confident that you're no longer a beginner and can handle some radical moves without too much danger of wiping out (I won't say *no* danger, because there's no such thing if you're really working your edge). And you want to know enough to recognize something that's really over your head so you don't commit career suicide.

Your job right now is to find the experiences, projects, jobs, classes, mentors, and team members that will push that edge further and further, and help you build the skills and muscles you'll need when you do eventually take on that big, hairy, make-or-break jump, whether that's a few years—or just a few weeks—away. (See Chapter 3: Going for Big Air, for more on how to plan your extreme career trajectory.) In the meantime, it's passion for the process that will keep you motivated.

NEXT UP ▸▸
What does it mean to be truly passionate about what you do?
And how do you make sure that happens?

END CHAPTER 1 ▪

PASSION IS ESSENTIAL TO A
TRULY EXTREME CAREER. IT'S
WHAT MOTIVATES YOU TO
PUSH BEYOND YOUR LIMITS. ▶

THEN FOLD, CREASE AND TEAR THIS ST

REMOVE SIDE EDGES

Fast Forward

Chapter 2
Get Stoked About What You Do—and Stay Stoked

AMP UP THE PASSION. ▶ Neal Lenarsky is an executive agent. That is to say, he finds the most ambitious and talented executives in the media, technology, fashion, and consumer-goods industries and creates opportunities for them the way other agents do for athletes and movie stars. It's a job he invented for himself back in 1996.

His first career had been in human resources, hiring executives into the Walt Disney Company, PepsiCo, and Guess, and sometimes helping them to adjust or move on after a company merger. Eventually he realized it wasn't entirely the right fit for him, so he began formulating his own next step. He decided that he wanted to help executives to analyze their careers and find the opportunities that would best suit them, but without having an employer's corporate agenda compromising his advice.

People who have truly extreme careers find a way to hold on to that total passion year in and year out.

Such a job didn't really exist, so he created his own extreme career helping high-performing people to find their passion and push their edge—something that excites him and motivates him to do his best work every day.

"I realized that the deep thought that goes into business doesn't go into career planning and management. People often let corporate forces steer their careers instead of steering their careers themselves," Lenarsky says.

If you're not strapping yourself into the driver's seat and actively steering your career, well, no one else is actively steering it, either. The result is that your career meanders instead of staying on a course. You feel totally pumped about what you do when you're twenty-five and everything is new and exciting, but you're burnt out, bummed out, and bored by the time you're forty because you've lost your sense of purpose and, with it, your self-motivation.

Lenarsky observes that the people who have truly extreme careers find a way to hold on to that total passion for what they do year in and year out. Being excited by and fully engaged in what you do goes hand in hand with the need to keep challenging your own abilities—they feed each other. The people he most likes working with are the people who have kept that passion or who want to regain it.

So, he spends a lot of time talking with new clients about how they can be more successful *and* how they can be happier and more satisfied. Sometimes it means a relatively small shift, like making the final push for a promotion one step up that will give them room to grow and stretch their muscles again. And sometimes it means taking a career in a whole new direction, such as leaving the corporate fold to start a new business or work independently on a series of projects.

For an example of how one person's career has been driven by passion, turn the page. ▶ **To find out how to stoke your own passion, skip ahead to page 052.** ▶▶

FOR_____

DATE_____

While You Were Out

TIME _____ A.M. P.M.

Urgent ☐

M_____

OF_____

PHONE_____

AREA CODE   NUMBER   EXTENSION

TELEPHONED		PLEASE CALL	
CAME TO SEE YOU		WILL CALL AGAIN	
RETURNED YOUR CALL		WANTS TO SEE YOU	

MESSAGE_____

_____

_____

_____

_____

_____

_____

SIGNED_____

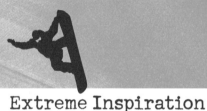

048

Alain Chuard *grew up in Switzerland, where kids learn to ski about the same time they learn to walk. That doesn't mean everyone is great at it or that everyone loves it; it just means everyone knows how to do it.*

Alain was okay at skiing and less than okay at most other sports until he started snowboarding in high school in the early 1990s. "I did it with ease and progressed quickly, and I noticed that if I worked hard and trained, I progressed even more," he recalls. It was the first time in his life that he felt really excited about something, and the first time he felt the urge to push himself. "It showed me if I work on myself and am driven, I can attain much more than I thought I could," he says.

That lesson—that having a passion for something can motivate you to push beyond yourself—has guided his snowboarding and his career.

He competed locally, then nationally (he was at one time ranked 14th in Switzerland), and went on to the World Cup, where he placed as high as 4th place. After two years of competing, he began to feel that snowboarding was the only thing in his life. This one-dimensionality didn't suit him, so he quit the competitive circuit and came to the U.S. to go to college, majoring in math and economics. Afterward all his friends were heading to Wall Street, so he followed.

"I really prepared for the interview process. Being a former pro snowboarder was helpful—it made me stand out from the usual analyst crowd," he says. But despite trying to bring the same focus and dedication to banking that he'd given to boarding, after his first year at Salomon Smith Barney, he wasn't feeling the love.

The hours were too long, the company had too many layers to climb up, and the work wasn't as interesting as he'd hoped.

Needing to reclaim some of the passion and self-motivation that he wasn't getting from work, Chuard returned to competitive snowboarding—qualifying for and competing in the U.S. half-pipe nationals during his second year at Solly—and he began looking around for a job that would have him feeling stoked off the snow, too.

The notion of starting a business crossed his mind...and kept crossing it. His father and other relatives had founded successful companies in Switzerland, and he found additional entrepreneurial role models among his investment-banking clients. "I saw a lot of people in investment banking who were too risk averse. And I saw companies that succeeded because of a few bright people who just did it."

Chuard decided he wanted to be one of the doers. He left Wall Street and headed out to Colorado to start a business that would combine his business acumen and snowboarding experience—an adventure travel company called Access Adventure Travel.

049

He and cofounder Victoria Ranson started the business in 2001 with the idea of providing active vacations for adults. The first was a snowboarding tour of New Zealand, where a troop of experts, including Chuard, would help travelers hone their style and skills. Inspired by the fun he had teaching at a snowboarding camp when he was younger, and by the experiences he had traveling for the World Cup, the just-past-thirty entrepreneur commented on his business plan, "I had a gut feeling it was a good combination for adults."

Instead of letting himself be shaped by a job that was coveted, prestigious, and well paying, but not his bag, Chuard held on to his individuality and held out for what was important to him—a situation where his passion for the work would motivate him to excel. And that was a job where he had more control over the business and a more direct impact on the customer. He notes, "I like running the tours and watching people do something they're interested in for two weeks. They get to see themselves progress and achieve something. It's very satisfying."

PASSION

+

MOTIVATION

=

EVEN MORE
PASSION

After slaloming through the obstacles of 9/11, the recession that followed, and the war in Iraq, which all took their toll on the travel business, Access finally began growing steadily enough that Chuard was able to step aside for two years to get his MBA, so he could keep his skills one step ahead of the company's progress. He chose Stanford Business School, where he knew he would find other entrepreneurs to teach and inspire him.

"When I think of extreme careers, I think of my boss at Salomon, who works one hundred hours a week and makes millions but has no quality of life," he explains. "On the other hand, in Silicon Valley I've met entrepreneurs who work just as hard as the guys on Wall Street but have extreme careers in a more positive sense. To take an idea and translate it into a real company that influences millions of people around the world—to me that's quite extreme."

He hopes to do just that with Access Adventure Travel. "If I were to remain an entrepreneur, that would be my dream, and that would be quite extreme."

051

HOW DO YOU GET STOKED ABOUT WHAT YOU DO—AND STAY STOKED? ▶
First up, take a time-out to zero in on what makes you feel excited about work and your career, and think about what will have you feeling equally stoked in the years to come. (Don't worry, no one expects you to be in your ultimate job right now.)

Unless you can envision these essentials, there's no way you can be true to yourself, your motivations, and your goals. If you can see these clearly now, you will be sure which opportunities to jump at and which ones to take a pass on when they come your way. (Remember: Saying no—even to things that might sound good on paper but don't fit your big picture—is part of maintaining your individuality.)

A lot of people, especially early on in their careers, define passion too simply. It's not just a matter of deciding that you love law or investing or fashion design or product development or publishing, and then doing it wherever or however you can.

052 Because, as you may have already discovered, you can love your profession but hate your day-to-day work for lots of different reasons. If the boss or the company or the team or the job is wrong for you, it can suck the passion and motivation right out of you. People who have taken their careers to an extreme level and who are motivated by their excitement for what they do know this. They make it a priority not only to love their work but to do it in a context they love, knowing that can change over time.

Take almost any profession, from recruiting to marketing to scientific research to accounting, and you can practice it in a variety of circumstances.

You can work for a big company or a small one or a not-for-profit or work for yourself.

You can have a hands-on, mentor boss or one who gives you a lot of autonomy.

You can be part of a tight, gung-ho, we-must-pound-beers-together-every-night team or a loose group where everyone works well together but goes their own way at 6 P.M.

053

You can seek out an organization that's going through major upheaval or rapid expansion or one that's all about steady growth.

Often you don't know what you do like until you work in a few situations that you don't. (That's what your twenties are for, so stick with the process but don't get stuck.) The important thing is to recognize when a situation isn't working for you and to understand why it isn't working, so that you can move on to something you're excited about every day. **Here's an example of someone who's found his niche.** ▸

Climb your way into the right niche

054

Bill Patton is the marketing director for Concept2, a Vermont rowing-machine maker, and a veteran rock climber and boulderer. After college, he spent nearly six years working his way back and forth across the country, skiing all winter and rock-climbing in the warm weather. He lived in a Volkswagen van, worked odd jobs, and perfected his raw ramen noodle–eating technique. And he climbed a lot of big walls, snagging a few first ascents.

It seems like the ultimate slacker life, but even then he had a clear goal—to climb as much as he possibly could. "It was a fairly disciplined lifestyle. You don't spend money on frivolous stuff when you're living on five hundred dollars a month," he points out.

It's also a situation where you spend a lot of time with yourself. You become very self-contained, self-directed, and self-motivated. You learn to know yourself well and to trust your own abilities.

Patton eventually returned to the workaday world, got his MBA, and steered himself into corporate marketing jobs at big companies like Polaroid. They seemed alluringly grown-up and responsible, but (not surprisingly) he found himself "inside, wearing a suit and tie, and miserable."

He'd been attracted to marketing because during his travels he spent a lot of time in sporting goods stores, often hanging out with the equipment companies' sales-people. "They always talked about the marketing guys and all the input they got [to contribute] into product development and markets, and I thought that sounded cool," he explains.

But being on a lower rung of a big company's ladder didn't allow him the opportunity to offer that kind of input or have the autonomy he was used to. So, he gravitated back toward the outdoor sports industry, which got him out of the suit and tie and among a team of coworkers who shared his interests, understood his motivations, and appreciated his work style. It also brought him into smaller and younger companies, where he had an increasingly bigger say in things as he worked his way toward his current job.

Looking back over his career, Patton reflects, "I like to sit close to the fire. In a big corporation, someone else is always sitting closer, making the big decisions about how to build the fire and what wood to put on. In a small business, I can sit really close to the fire. And I value that."

He was right to think that marketing would suit him. Climbing big walls and boulders is all about strategizing and problem solving. When you can't get past a certain point on the wall, you have to back away, think the situation through, and find a new way to approach that route or find a different path.

Marketing uses those same problem-solving skills. "When marketing is done right, you're the connector between engineering [or product development] and sales and finance," explains Patton. And your job is to help each of those groups support the others, solving the problems that get in the way of coordinating their very different goals.

Though Patton was able to pick the right profession, the now forty-something executive wasn't able to find his groove and make the most of his abilities until he found a setting where he could reclaim some of the autonomy and self-direction he'd had while living on the road. "We have the Concept2 way of doing things. We believe that the conventional way...is not necessarily the best way. There's always room for improvement."

Common Threads

Patton might seem to have had a somewhat patchwork career, but in a world where everyone ultimately works for him- or herself, and work can be seen as a series of projects, few career paths are obvious beelines toward a fixed point. (The ones that are tend to be kinda dull.)

Look for the common threads: What was Bill Patton working toward as he made his way through his various jobs and titles? He was seeking work that he liked to do (marketing), with people he wanted to work with (other outdoors enthusiasts), and in an environment that made the best use of his skills and work style (a small company). Concept2 fits, and it's a young company so there's room for him to grow with it. What are the common threads in your career path so far? And where will they take you? This quiz will help you decide.

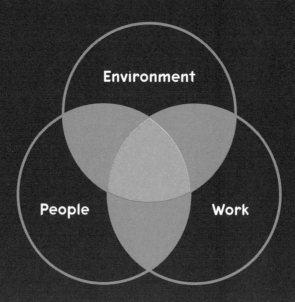

WHAT GETS YOU STOKED? FIFTEEN QUESTIONS ▶ Sometimes the things that motivate you and get you super-psyched aren't what you think they'll be—or even what you want them to be. So, be straight with yourself here (no one but you will see your answers). If you can't own up to what you want, you won't make it happen. So what if your friends are fast-talking salespeople? If crunching numbers behind the scenes is where it's at for you, commit to it and see where it takes you. You don't need to worry about anybody's passion but your own.

1. **What attracted you to your first job or two? (If you're just graduating from college, you can write about internships or summer jobs.) What were your expectations? Compare that with what you actually liked and disliked once you had the job. How do they match up?**

2. **When you were twenty-two, where did you want to be in ten years? Is that still what you want? If not, what's changed and why?**

3. Name one thing you expected to like or be good at, that turned out to be not so cool or left you floundering.

4. Name one thing that you dreaded or thought you would totally suck at that you tried and ended up excelling at and loving every minute.

5. You're at a party and someone asks what you do. Is it important that they immediately recognize the field you work in or the brand you work for and admire it? Or would it be satisfying to do something so ahead of the curve—or just slightly obscure—you're sure to get a blank look and have to explain?

6. Do you associate big companies with bankable prestige, resources, and opportunities or bureaucracy, politics, and occasional layoffs?

7. Do you associate start-ups with highly motivated people, innovation, and the chance to be part of something new and exciting or with chaos, meager resources, modest paychecks, and people who can't deal with having a boss?

8. Think of the best boss you ever had. What did you like about his or her work style? Which moves would you rip off if you held that position?

059

9. Think of the worst boss you ever had. What made him or her so lame? What did you learn *not* to do from this experience?

10. What was the coolest project you ever worked on? (The one that left you exhausted but definitely psyched and even reluctant to go home at the end of the day). What was so gratifying about it?

11. What project made you lie in bed every morning, not wanting to start your day? We're talking about the assignment that left you moaning, "Man, when will this be over!" What made it so unbearable?

12. If you work from home, do you feel productive and happy to be entirely in charge of your day and your distractions? Or do you feel isolated, unmotivated, disorganized, and way too distracted—by TV, the Internet, the cookie jar, your partner, kids, or pets, that picture you've been meaning to hang—everything but work, that is?

13. Do you feel energized during team meetings, or do they just feel like huge time-drains? Would you rather be handed your assignment and left alone to get it done?

14. When you dress for work, do you want to wear a snappy suit, straight-off-the-runway fashions, office casual, or your gym clothes?

061

15. Do you need to absolutely make the most money possible all the time, or is very good money good enough? Do you prefer the predictability of a steady paycheck or thrive on the possible upside of commissions, stock options, or other kinds of compensation?

YOUR ANSWERS ▸ For this quiz, there are no right answers. What's important is that you *have* answers to all these questions.

It's about taking the time to garner experiences and do some honest soul-searching so you can find work and a career path that truly motivate you. Otherwise, what's the point?

If you have definite answers and they confirm that you're in the right place for you to learn and grow and push your edge—excellent. But keep in mind that if the hill you're on now gets skied out—your opportunities to grow and learn start to shrink—you can use these answers to remind yourself about what drives and motivates you and where you're trying to get to, so that you make solid choices.

If everything about your current job leaves you way short of excited and only marginally motivated, use these questions to help you understand why. And consider the possibility that as much as a situation *appeals* to you, it might not actually *work* for you. Then get busy finding a new work situation that does.

IDENTIFY YOUR PERSONAL "NO-FALL ZONE." ▸ If you're lucky, whatever it is that isn't working will be obvious. These days, when so much job-hopping is the norm, sooner or later, everyone lands in his or her personal "no-fall zone." In the world of free skiing, that's a particularly treacherous stretch where you can't afford to make any miscalculations or you'll fall, and falling will cost you the race—or worse. In the work world, your no-fall zone is a situation you can't afford to fall into. It's a total deal breaker, completely unacceptable to you, and where you want *out*…yesterday.

If you find that you've fallen into a no-fall rut, don't despair. Almost everyone has a story of tumbling into the wrong work situation. The trick is getting out in one piece once you realize it. **Consider the following people who faced their no-fall zones and came out clean on the other side.** ▸

Your Career Is an Extreme Sport

NO-FALL ZONE

Goodbye, distant horizon; hello, instant gratification

Risa Shimoda *is a former whitewater kayaker who has represented the U.S. in four World Freestyle Championships, and an entrepreneur who now owns her own marketing company. She graduated from Stanford with a B.A. in mechanical engineering and landed a job at Procter & Gamble in a department that designed equipment needed to manufacture new products, like the machine that gives Pringles their distinctive shape and texture. For someone whose undergrad work emphasized product development, it was a pretty sweet gig. "I still think it's the coolest department," she says.*

"My job was to create the sleeves on a surgical gown that would be sewed together in a factory seven years hence," recalls Shimoda. For a woman who thrives on the speed and immediacy of navigating class-5 rapids, such delayed gratification was a no-fall zone. "I couldn't imagine waiting that long to see something through."

She scouted around for other jobs at P&G, and eventually moved over to marketing. "It was still product-oriented, so it wasn't a big leap," Shimoda says. But creating packaging, advertising, and promotions for finished products meant looking ahead months instead of years, which made it "a good fit" for her temperament as well as her skills.

Taking control by becoming the boss

Rick Alden *spent two years of his primarily self-employed career working for someone else. After selling Device, his snowboard equipment company, he took a hiatus from the entrepreneurial life to design fly-fishing rods for Orvis. Despite the appeal of a regular paycheck—his first as an adult—and the relief of not having to be in charge of everything all the time, he left after only a short time because he couldn't deal with not taking charge.*

Not long after he started at Orvis, financial problems in another part of the business led to layoffs across the company, including in his department. He survived. But "because of a problem that had nothing to do with us, people around me were getting fired. I suddenly discovered the fear and insecurity of having someone else in control of my fate."

That was his no-fall zone.

He left Orvis and used the money he made selling Device to fund Skullcandy, which put him back in his zone. "People always ask if it's scary to be an entrepreneur without the security of a big company behind you. But I don't mind failing—I just want it to be my failure. If I'm in trouble, I want it to be something I created for myself."

065

Saying no to a borderline-abusive boss

Benjamin Wagner's no-fall zone took human form: his boss at the website where he wrote and produced news for one short year before coming to MTV News.

"He gave me my first full-time job and my foot in the door, but he made me want to strangle him," Wagner recalls. "He was a yeller who motivated through fear. He was all old-school caffeinated newsroom bluster, and it was too much negative energy."

Under the pressure of covering the 1996 Democratic National Convention in Chicago, where his boss's temper "bubbled up to a level that bordered on abusive," Wagner decided he'd had enough. "I could take you to the exact spot on Lakeshore Drive where I decided I was out of there—that it wasn't the environment I wanted to work in," he says.

A few days after he returned to New York from Chicago, a friend told him about an opening at MTV News working for someone he'd met (and seen keep cool under pressure) in the pressroom at the convention. Wagner applied and accepted the job. He says, "I rarely have a bad day here."

Of course, just as extreme athletes need to keep their cool and perform when weather, equipment, or aggressive competitors are bumming them out, extreme careerists have to keep centered and figure out how to rise above a bad work situation.

You *do* get something out of everything.

The fact is, you *do* get something out of everything—and there was *some* reason why you took that oh-so-lame job to begin with. So, while you're camping out in your no-fall zone, think about one thing you want to get out of it and one thing you want to tell people you achieved. Focus on those things to stay motivated and on top of your game. And remember that exiting with grace is one thing that divides extreme winners from intolerable whiners. Move on as soon as you can find a job that motivates you to rock, and gives you the opportunity to rock—but not a second sooner.

067

NEXT UP ▸▸
Work is practice and work is training. Building toward your big air.

END CHAPTER 2 ■

An extreme career isn't
about working toward
a single ultimate goal.
It's about pulling off awe-
inspiring tricks with awesome
style, again and again.

REMOVE SIDE EDGES FIRST
AND TEAR THIS STUB ALONG PERFORATION

Chapter 3

Going for Big Air:
Extreme Career Paths

071

THERE'S MORE THAN ONE SUMMIT—AND MANY ROUTES TO THE TOP. ▶
Your father and possibly your mother most likely made their way along singular
and straightforward career paths, probably toward lofty titles that became the
pinnacles of their corporate trajectories—like a climber who believes there's
only one mountain to summit and one route to the top.

That strategy is so old-school. It has nothing to do with how you and your
peers are going to build successful careers today.

Sure, if you work in a traditional field—law, accounting, consulting, or
investment banking—your goals still are likely to include becoming a partner
or managing director. These are tangible, fixed points to corral your skills and
experience toward. But even these goals aren't the straight ascent they once
were. A person might move among different departments or practice groups, or

You need to play the skateboarder or snowboarder, building your career on a series of progressively complex tricks.

even leave firm life to work for some other kind of company or strike out on their own, perhaps returning to firm work later.

In creative, science, and technology fields, in particular, but also consulting, finance, and other professions, few extreme careerists play the mountain climber, striving to bag one singular, impressive peak to culminate their career.

No way. Instead, you need to play the skateboarder or snowboarder, building your career on a series of progressively complex tricks that further your skills, give you a major high, and impress the hell out of anyone watching you.

Your career is about big air. And anyone who rides any kind of board for a living knows you can grab big air more than once in your lifetime. If you're really good at what you do, and if you practice a lot, you will astound over and over again.

Your awe-inspiring feats are of a slightly different nature from a snowboarder's, of course. They are the projects, promotions, and other challenges that collectively comprise a career. Each one should serve a purpose—to expose you to people or experience or an organization you're interested in, or to enable you to build skills that you need. Or they should showcase skills and experience you've been working on that you want people to associate with you.

So, instead of stating one or two singular long-term peaks you want to summit, your career plan should consist of a list of ambitious achievements (the cool tricks) that you think would be amazing to accomplish. They might include working for an innovative company you admire or with a superstar in your line of work. These accomplishments could include awards you'd like to win, or types of projects you'd like to work on or head up, or a line of business somewhere in

your company that you want to be exposed to, or a series of jobs you'd love to have the chance to try your hand at.

Some of these feats might need to be done in a particular order (easier before harder), but others can be taken on when the opportunity presents itself (or when you create it).

No, they won't take you along a singular path toward an ultimate *destination*. But if you're clear about why you're taking on each challenge and what you want to get out of it, then they'll move your career forward and give it the shape and *direction* you want it to take. Each target should be impressive and worthwhile in its own right—and it should have you grabbing big air.

As you accomplish one goal, more opportunities will likely surface, giving you the option of continuing further in one direction or shifting toward something new. (If that isn't happening, you probably have your eyes wide shut.) Like an athlete who's just won his or her toughest competition yet, you should keep adding new, more ambitious goals to your list. This keeps you pushing your edge further out, and it keeps you engaged, challenged, and, yes, *stoked* about your work.

ll A CAREER BASED ON AWE-INSPIRING MOVES

About halfway though a dazzling career that started when he was twelve, Tony Hawk made a list of things he wanted to accomplish as a pro skater. It didn't include designing video games, owning a skating gear company, running a skateboard exhibition tour, being a special guest on *The Simpsons*, or hosting a radio show. It was just a list of tricks that he had never done—in fact, some of them had never been done by anyone. They included something called an ollie 540 and a 900-degree spin. With this list to focus his efforts and motivate him, he entered more than 100 pro contests—and won seventy-three of them. That dedication drew a lot of attention his way, opening up all those other opportunities. When he checked off the last feat on the list, the 900, at the 1999 X Games, he shifted the emphasis of his career, retiring from competition to focus on those entrepreneurial challenges and the new tricks that came with them.

073

Career Path

goal

Your Parents

You

Extreme Inspiration

Making a career of changing careers

● New York

● California   ● South Africa

Frank Karbe *is a few years shy of forty, an Ironman triathlete, and the CFO of Exelixis, a San Francisco biotech company.*

076

He is doing exactly what he wants to be doing, but he certainly didn't get there by a slow and steady climb up the proverbial corporate ladder. He ended up in this cool job by way of a series of careers that were each purposefully chosen and that opened up appealing and challenging opportunities that weren't entirely foreseeable at the time he took the plunge.

After finishing business school in Germany, Karbe was interested in finance but not sure he wanted to commit to the unending hours of the average investment banking gig. He took a corporate finance job at Royal Dutch/Shell instead, where he made good progress. But he knew he wouldn't spend his whole career there. "I remember during one of my reviews, at the top of the page it said, 'natural retirement date: 2033,' and I couldn't contemplate being there that long. Variety is the spice of life, you know?"

A few years later, his wife moved to New York to get her MBA. Shell did not have an outpost there, so he saw an opportunity to try something new. Frank Karbe reconsidered investment banking because most firms have big New York offices. Although his motives weren't entirely career-driven, he had a clear purpose for pursuing this new path and that guided the firm he chose (Goldman Sachs), the deal he made (they promised to pay for relocating him), and the work and people he sought out once he started.

Ironically, the relocation didn't come through until it was almost time for his wife to return to Frankfurt, but in the meantime, Karbe "turned out to like investment

banking and to be good at it." So, he shifted his attention away from corporate finance and began working on grabbing big air as a banker.

The first ramp he had to clear: few people move from corporate jobs into investment banking (more move the other way), so as a first-year associate, he had second- and third-year analysts working for him who had more banking experience than he did, and absolutely no one else shared his corporate experience.

"I told my analysts that they knew more about some things than I did, but maybe I knew some things they didn't, too," he recalls.

He observed the people around and under him to see what new skills he needed, and he made sure his peers and superiors valued the knowledge and tools he brought with him. "I would try to bring my own perspective to the table and provide analysis that other people weren't seeing that I thought was valuable," he says.

Karbe also made a deal with himself when he took the job at Goldman: He wouldn't be one of those bankers who let work consume them completely, just so they could retire at thirty-five. "You never know if that will really happen, so I refused to not do the things I wanted to do in my personal life," he says.

I was viewed as the guy who sailed around the world, and it shaped people's impression of me.

On a break from his high-powered deal making, in South Africa in 1997, he saw the yachts from the BT round-the-world sailing race pull into Cape Town to finish one of the toughest legs of their journey. He saw crew members disembarking with a mixture of pride, accomplishment, and disbelief on their faces—along with a clear appreciation for one another. He immediately knew he wanted to be a part of that. The fact that he'd never sailed before wasn't important. He signed up, got on a crew, and began flying to the U.K. for weekend training in the north Atlantic. His ship, the Quadstone, eventually started to gear up for the 2000–01 race.

"I had to tell Goldman I needed several months off to sail around the world," he says. Friends told him he was crazy—Goldman Sachs doesn't normally give people time off to go play with boats. But he had a fallback plan: If they didn't grant his request he'd quit. Luckily the firm gave him the time off to pursue this life-shaping experience he wanted to have. They even sponsored his ship.

He sailed the South Seas, facing down brutal storms that conjured eighty-foot waves and winds so strong "you'd need ski goggles just to be able to open your eyes on deck." At one point the sail was damaged and had to be repaired in the middle of the night. His ship pulled into Cape Town in early 2001, nearly four years to the day after he decided he wanted to try ocean sailing.

When he returned to Goldman Sachs, to his naysayers' surprise, he discovered the time off hadn't hurt him; instead it gave him new leadership capabilities and insights, and possibly increased his stature within the company.

The life-or-death experience of navigating the high seas gave him confidence in his ability to handle any situation. "When I had to walk into a boardroom to give a presentation, instead of being nervous because [I didn't] know what [was] going to happen, I saw it as an opportunity and was able to enjoy the experience," he recalls.

The fact that he completed the race changed coworkers' perceptions of him. "[I was viewed] not just as what I did at the office but as a whole person. I was viewed as the guy who sailed around the world, and it shaped people's impression of me," Karbe explains.

It enhanced a growing reputation he had for being able to dive into new situations and manage them well, and it probably helped Karbe garner an offer to work in San Francisco for a short spell—which he took, of course. Once there, he and his wife liked the west coast, so he asked for a permanent transfer. He tacked in a new direction yet again, trading in European blue chip firms for Silicon Valley start-ups, and began building the new relationships with coworkers and clients that he'd need to grab big air in a new business environment.

Karbe was successful enough that one of his clients, Exelixis, offered him a job as their CFO. People again told him he was crazy and asked how he could leave Goldman

Sachs after all the time he'd put in there. But this was an opportunity for him to get funding for a biotech company and help it get its first products to market (talk about grabbing big air!). "It seemed exciting to me. We could be the next Microsoft or Genentech," he says.

So at thirty-five, instead of thinking about taking early retirement from banking, Karbe charted yet another new course for himself. He gave up the prestige and financial prosperity he'd have gained as a managing director at a large investment bank, but he also opened up some exciting new opportunities for himself. "After we make Exelixis successful, I'd like to be a CEO one day," he says.

That would be some major air.

SOMETIMES WORK IS PRACTICE FOR BIG AIR; SOMETIMES IT'S THE VERTICAL WHERE YOU GRAB IT. ▶ Serious snowboarders tend to cluster on prime snow hills and skateboarders do the same in skate parks. It's where they try new moves and push their edges and often fall on their asses. And it's where they learn from each other, egg each other on, and give one another other props when they pull off an aggressive trick with awesome style.

Your job is your skate park. It's where you find coaches to help you figure things out and work through your trouble spots, and peers and role models to teach you new tricks and flawless style. It's where you literally *practice* your profession.

There are times when you choose a job or a project because it offers new training—the chance to learn a new skill or develop specific muscles. Other times the opportunity at hand is the big one you've been practicing for. It's your X Games and you want to show that you can pull off your own 450-degree spins with fluidity, confidence, and ease.

When Trey Gregory was training to become a professional free skier he was skiing 135 days a year—pretty much every second he could. He spent a lot of that time with people he knew were more experienced and more skilled then he was. He watched their techniques and practiced them himself. Trying to keep up pushed him to get better fast. Gradually he felt his skills and his muscles develop to the point where he was willing to test them in competitions.

Now that he's in a new game, public relations, he's going through the same process—pushing himself to excel in a new arena quickly. At client meetings he observes senior coworkers' styles and techniques. He pays attention to other peoples' good ideas in strategy meetings, and seeks feedback on his press releases and strategy briefs—all in an effort to develop the skills he needs to be a capable hired counselor.

"You want to know that the foundation and the muscle memory are there, so you're confident that you can survey a situation and…make the right decisions." On this new hillside, that means "walking into the office of the chief marketing officer of a $4 billion company believing that I can understand his company and give him the right recommendations and advice."

What's big air for him? "I'd like to be the guy who hires the public relations guy," he says, which means going "in-house," possibly in a public relations or marketing role, where he can tackle "big picture" issues, like the marketing and branding strategies for a large company. "That person is more in the driver's seat than the outside guy who gives advice," he explains.

You can't always anticipate the coolest opportunities that will come your way (as Frank Karbe's career demonstrates). But if you aren't out there pulling your best moves in venues where important people can see what you've got, opportunities won't come your way and you won't have the currency to create them either.

Your job is your skate park. It's where you find coaches to help 081 **you work through your trouble spots. It's where you literally *practice* your profession.**

CREATE YOUR EXTREME-CAREER TRAINING PROGRAM. ▶ Creating a list of ways you'd like to grab some big air can help you think about the skills you're ready to show off, the muscles you still need to develop, and how you plan to build them. Use this worksheet to help you.

List three to five things that would be big air for you. (They could be projects or jobs, specific mentors or companies, or an entirely new career path.)

Choose the one goal you'd like to achieve next, and answer the following questions: What is your biggest barrier to bagging this opportunity?

Name one thing that's in your power to do right now to create this opportunity for yourself.

Should you get a chance to grab this big air, what skills, knowledge, or contacts would you need to nail it?

Which of those things do you have down?

Which do you need to work on?

How can you use your current job to gain that experience or build those muscles?

Who (at your company or elsewhere) can be a coach, providing guidance or advice that would be helpful to you?

List two milestones that will move you closer to grabbing big air. What are realistic deadlines for hitting them?

You need to recognize situations that could be opportunities, and understand how to pursue them and shape them into what you want them to be.

GOING FOR THE WHOLE SHOT. ▸ Occasionally opportunity drops in your lap (like Frank Karbe's offer from Exelixis), and sometimes you need to carve it out for yourself in a place where there doesn't seem to be anything going on (by starting a new company, for example). But most often you need to recognize situations that *could* be opportunities, and understand how to pursue them and shape them into what you want them to be.

John Allen has built his career on doing just that. It wasn't too long after Allen lost his training wheels that he traded in his bicycle for something with more throttle. He has been riding competitive motocross since he was ten. By the time he was fifteen he'd broken his femur three times (placing third in the race the last time around, he makes sure to note). Sometime around the age of forty he shattered his elbow. But that hasn't dampened his enthusiasm for this loud, fast, and extremely physical sport. Three decades of bumps and bruises and breaks have only given him a keen appreciation for *the whole shot*.

Getting the whole shot is a motocross term that means grabbing the best position on the track right out of the gate. You're out in front and on your own instead of jostling with all the other racers for position. It's an opportunity you see and you grab because it sets you apart from the pack, literally, and gives you a huge advantage for as long as you can hold onto it (though, if you fall, look out—you will have a pile of bikes riding roughshod over you.)

Off the track, Allen is a wealth advisor for Merrill Lynch in Sacramento, California. Wealth management may sound like a surprisingly tame job, but he points out, "You go for the kill in this business. Most of my clients came from some other firm, so it's competitive. You're always out meeting people and building your business."

When you don't have to win your clients from someone else, when they're uncommitted and up for grabs, that's a whole shot. And Allen is well practiced in knowing how to spot opportunities, chase them down, and use them to his advantage.

He reads tech magazines, newspapers, and local business journals, and works with groups like the Sacramento Angels and the Sacramento Area Regional Technology Alliance, so he's the first to hear about venture capitalists raising new funds, companies going public or being bought, and executives exercising their options or retiring. "We want to see money in motion," he explains, because that's when people have decisions to make and are most open to hiring (or changing) advisors.

085

Each time Allen catches the attention of someone with great net worth and snags a meeting, he's grabbed the whole shot. How does he know he's made the most of it? "When I walk out of a meeting and I know I nailed it. I know I got the prospect thinking about what I had to say," he says. But the big air comes "when I get them to sign the papers to work with me."

There are all kinds of ways to grab the whole shot. Consider the following two tales. ▶

Listening when opportunity knocks

Robyn Benincasa is an adventure racer whose team placed first in the 2000 Eco-Challenge and the 1998 Raid Gauloises. At an appearance she'd made for one of her sponsors, a woman approached her and asked if she'd considered talking to corporate audiences about teamwork. Benincasa hadn't but immediately saw the potential for big air. She developed a PowerPoint presentation with eight lessons about teamwork, and illustrated each one with video footage from her races. She let this woman book a few gigs for her but eventually started her own company, World Class Teams, and has since worked with Nestlé, Key Bank, Timberland, and Starbucks.

086   She says, "It's cool to go into a Starbucks store and have the workers recite my presentation back to me. They tell me, 'We're building human synergy right now!'"

Spotting opportunity and going for it

Risa Shimoda cut her marketing teeth at Procter & Gamble, a company known equally for its category-dominating consumer brands and for its conservative, stratified work environment. When she moved to Mars Inc. to work on the M&M's brand, this highly individualistic kayaker observed "a very flat, entrepreneurial environment. Ideas moved through the building quickly." She took advantage of that by jumping on the opportunity to sponsor the 1984 Winter Olympic Games when it was offered. "The company had no preconceptions ... They told me to go find out what I could. Then I had to sell it to them and get the project pushed through." The campaign, which featured ads with known Olympians, marked the beginning of Mars' effort to reposition M&M's as a snack food (instead of a confection).

Through this campaign, Shimoda helped to raise M&M's profile—and her own. She used that to get her next job, at the Coca-Cola Company, where anyone interested in learning to build and sustain a global brand wants to spend some time.

SALE

0712600314832005032

DO YOU NEED TO TAKE IT DOWN A NOTCH? ▸ Even amateurs who train for major endurance events like a marathon, an ultra run, or an Ironman competition hire coaches. They do it to help them train smartly and make the most of their prep work. But often the most valuable thing the coach can help them do is learn when to rest or take it easy so they don't over-train and either injure themselves or wear themselves out before a big race.

Professional trainers make sure the athletes' strongest traits, like aggressiveness, persistence, and focus, don't completely take over and work against them. Coaches keep athletes balanced by helping them cultivate personal qualities that are equally important but come less readily, like patience and an ability to pull back and take in the big picture.

Kayaker Risa Shimoda has nearly unlimited risk tolerance and fearlessness. These traits allowed her to paddle the gorge below Niagara Falls and become the first woman to descend the Green River Narrows in North Carolina.

They've served her well in her career, too, giving her the wherewithal to move all over the eastern U.S., trading up to bigger, more challenging marketing jobs, and then leave the corporate life for a spell to launch a sports-themed greeting card company.

> **"There are risks to not being afraid. You don't always go in as prepared as you should be."**

But that doesn't mean those qualities are always good. "I wish I were more fearful, but it's not part of my personality....There are risks to not being afraid. You don't always go in as prepared as you should be."

If you're not self-aware when you try to pull off an awe-inspiring feat, instead of grabbing big air, you'll do a major face-plant.

Case in point, when American Whitewater, a not-for-profit organization that promotes river conservation and public river access for recreation, asked

36.00
3.11
1 @ 6.99
0.60
1 @ 6.99
0.60
1 @ 6.99
0.60
56.97
4.91

087

Shimoda to be its executive director, she said yes. She was familiar with the group from her years of kayaking and was confident that if there were parts of the job she didn't know well, she'd be able to figure them out as she went along.

But Shimoda hadn't fully appreciated how big a part of the job fund-raising would be, or how little she understood the dynamics of that world. "Right after I began, the [stock] market crashed, which affects how much people and organizations can give. So, right as I was starting to go out and ask for support, people had no support to give." As a result, she had to spend more of her time adjusting the organization to its shrinking budget. "It became wearying," she says. She left after a short time to return to more familiar waters, starting her own marketing firm, the Shimoda Group.

She avoided a total wipeout, but by not doing enough research and planning, she essentially had to bail out before even trying for big air.

In retrospect she observes, "It was risky, going from for-profit to not-for-profit; it was a big change. I don't know whether it was naïveté or not being afraid that made me think I could just go do it."

She's unlikely to try to shake the risk tolerance and lack of fear that have mostly served her well—and she shouldn't. But experience has made her more aware of how they can also undermine her. "I know I can manage the adversity that potentially comes with taking risks and I get confidence from that," she says, "but I do more planning now."

What strengths do you possess that could possibly be your undoing? Use this table to help you avoid overdoing it.

0881152666

KEEP THIS RECEIPT

FOR RETURN/EXCHANGE

How to keep your killer instinct from killing you

If you excel at...	Be sure to practice...
Taking risks	Researching and planning, so you understand what you're undertaking.
Being focused	Pulling back to appreciate the bigger picture of what you're trying to achieve.
Being aggressive	Being empathetic, so you can read people and know when you're ticking them off.
Being persistent and resilient	Being patient, to appreciate when sitting and waiting will help you more than pushing ahead.
Being an individual	Working with others, because even in this self-driven climate, you need them.

NEXT UP ▶▶
You've grabbed all the big air you can in your current job.
Time to scope out new opportunities?

TAKING YOUR CAREER TO THE EXTREME MEANS TAKING AN HONEST INVENTORY AND HOLDING OUT FOR WORK SITUATIONS THAT WILL TRULY PUSH YOUR EDGE. ▶

REMOVE SIDE EDGES FIRST AND TEAR THIS STUB ALONG PERFORATION

Chapter 4
What's Next?
Sizing Up Opportunities

093

WHERE TO CATCH YOUR PERFECT WAVE. ▶ Matt Jacobson, a television production executive recently turned free agent in his early forties, is also a lifetime surfer who grew up in southern California. He's surfed all over the world and is experienced enough to know what his priorities are when it comes to catching some awesome waves. "I'd rather surf mediocre surf with friends than catch the perfect wave all by myself," he says.

An excellent surfing session: A few years ago he traveled to Bali where a movie-director friend had a house on a remote part of the island, well away from Bali's most famous and crowded surfer beaches. "It was the first time in a long time I could surf with just friends for four or five hours, until you're [almost] too tired to even paddle back in," he says. He'd relive that day anytime.

Taking your career to the extreme means holding out for positions that will add something significant to your portfolio of experiences.

Tahiti was a different story. The scene is all about reef surfing, one of the latest attempts to make surfing—one of the original extreme sports—even more extreme. "I had to swim a half mile out to get to the reef, then I hit my head on it before I even got a wave in. It was chaotic—not my scene. I just paddled back in," he recounts.

One of his favorite places to surf is in So-Cal—literally in his own backyard. "I can go out and catch a couple of waves in twenty minutes and feel great. I have friends who spend all their time driving up and down the coast looking for the perfect wave. They always get skunked. They'd get more surfing in if they just stayed put."

Take a cue from Jacobson on keeping perspective: His attitude is as applicable to your career path as it is to a surfer's pipe dreams.

As noted in the introduction, the average time spent in a job these days is four to six years. If you're awesome at what you do, and if you're good at showcasing your skills to the right people, then even more job offers than that are likely to come your way—perhaps many more.

Of course, not every offer is one that you'll want to accept. Taking your career to the extreme means holding out for positions that will add something significant to your portfolio of experiences; the right job should give you plenty of opportunities to build new skills and to apply your abilities in a challenging environment.

Essentially, you want to develop a system of analyzing situations that will help you size up current and potential jobs the way Jacobson looks at his surfing opportunities—and, you should be able to trust your gut. Sometimes the job you already have is your best chance for catching the most awesome waves, and you're better off passing up other offers to stay put. At other times the waves really will be bigger and badder at the beach up the road.

You also want to be able to tell when a beach is surfed out for you and it's just time to move on. Even CEOs, the men and women at the top of their game, can stay in a job too long, unnecessarily damaging their reputations. Steve Mader, vice chairman for the search firm Christian & Timbers, who has made a career of identifying and placing top executives, observes, "I've seen CEOs get fired, and it's not because they're suddenly not effective leaders any longer. It's just that their moment is over. The organization has evolved and they're not the right fit."

If you're overstaying your usefulness, you're not pushing your edge. So, taking your career to the extreme means taking an honest inventory and recognizing when it's time to chase down the next wave—or risk getting dragged down by the undertow.

095

This chapter provides a set of tools to help you size up your current gig and think about what you want from your next one, so you can make informed, self-aware decisions about where you're likely to find your perfect wave at this moment in time. If the wheels are already in motion, it also provides questions and tips that will help you compare and evaluate current opportunities.

HOW TO KNOW THE RIGHT WAVE WHEN YOU SEE IT. ▶ Like Jacobson and his Tahitian reef, sometimes a job just isn't working for you and it's time to move on to something that suits you better. And sometimes you have no reason to leave a place, but an alluring offer comes along. Ideally every move you make should balance the push and pull: You want to be clear about what you're leaving *and* what you're moving to, and why you're doing both.

Check out the following career trajectories; these extreme careerists were clear about where they had been and where they were going each time they made a new move.

David Becker
Career: Marketing
The moves: Franklin Templeton Investments ▸▸ Intuit ▸▸ Frog Design ▸▸ Philippe Becker Design
The motivation: The opportunity to combine his business acumen and tech savvy in a setting where he could support creative people.
His evaluation: "After financial services, high tech was vastly mind-expanding. It was like getting in the Wonkavator; you could go in any direction. Frog offered more of that and Becker offers even more still."

Frank Karbe

Career: Finance

The moves: Royal Dutch/Shell ▸▸ Goldman Sachs ▸▸ Exelixis

The motivation: A change of environment and new challenges that Karbe believed he could balance with his personal interests (i.e., running triathlons and sailing around the world).

His evaluation: "I never tried that hard to be anything in particular, and maybe because of that interesting things happened. Most people join Goldman Sachs to become a partner; I joined to go to New York. So I had a different agenda. That perhaps made me stand apart."

097

Risa Shimoda

Career: Marketing

The moves: Procter & Gamble ▸▸ Mars ▸▸ Coca-Cola

The motivation: Broader responsibilities each time, and the chance to work on strong brands that still had room to grow.

Her evaluation: "In [each of] these jobs I was in a situation where I was working on something different or new or that seemed peripheral to the main business, but I was given a lot of latitude to pursue what I thought were good opportunities for the brand."

If you're no longer inspired by the waves you've been surfing and your gut is saying that you're ready for your next challenge, answer these questions *before* you start scouting for something new. Then match each and every new opportunity against the priorities you checked off in these lists.

1. What do you want from a new job that you aren't getting now? (Check as many as apply.)
- ❏ a good boss
- ❏ coworkers who challenge and support me (more team)
- ❏ more acknowledgement and reward for my individual talents and successes (less team)
- ❏ a change in the content of my day-to-day work
- ❏ a different company culture
- ❏ more responsibility
- ❏ more money
- ❏ a new geographic location
- ❏ a change in lifestyle
- ❏ other: _____

2. What aspects of your current job would you take with you if you could?
- ❏ my boss
- ❏ my colleagues
- ❏ my corporate resources
- ❏ the brand I work on
- ❏ my day-to-day activities
- ❏ my benefits
- ❏ my lifestyle
- ❏ the company culture
- ❏ my clients
- ❏ my hours
- ❏ other: _____

SCOPE OUT COMPETITIVE BEACHES: HOW'S THE SURF AND WHAT ARE THE HAZARDS? ▸ These two questions should help you to think about what you want, and what you want to avoid, in your next gig. Once you have an opportunity (or even better, a few of them) in your sights, scope them out thoroughly. You want the job that will offer not just more money or prestige (those things should be a given) but an environment where you can take your career—and yourself—in a new direction. Once you're clear where the best opportunity is, focus on making all the right moves to ensure the sweetest possible offer.

What's the perfect deal and what's a real deal breaker?

The answer is subjective; it depends on where you are in your career and comfort zone. Some people are willing to put up with a situation that's far from ideal if there's a killer opportunity at the end of the tunnel that they don't think they can get anywhere else. Others believe that if they aren't totally happy they won't do their best work, and they won't make life harder than it has to be when they have the talent and skills to land a job that's satisfying all around.

For example, after graduating from U.C.L.A., Matt Jacobson accepted a job buying television airtime at an ad agency, even though he knew he didn't want to stay in advertising. He stuck with it for "exactly one year, one month, and one day," because there was a specific thing he wanted to get out it: He thought it would be a good introduction to the business side of television. He recalls, "It was a pretty crappy job, but I loved it. My boss was this fierce negotiator. She taught me how to value media and how to get the best deal for your client without burning people."

Having learned the lessons he wanted to, he moved on as quickly as he could to where he really wanted to be—on the business side of entertainment.

As he wound his way through increasingly bigger television production and development jobs at the Walt Disney Company, News Corporation, Broadcom, and Quiksilver, he developed a good instinct for what did and didn't work for him, and he listened to his gut when deciding which offers to accept and which to turn down. He explains, "There are always deals where people are telling you it's okay if it sucks a little. But if it doesn't feel right, it won't go right. You have to be able to say, 'It's just not gonna work' and walk away."

099

Ask yourself these questions about an opportunity you're considering and listen to what your instincts have to say about your answers:

What about this opportunity appeals to you?

What about this opportunity could potentially suck?

What are the big questions about this opportunity that you still need answered?

Extreme Inspiration

A career path driven by learning opportunities

Dave Alberga is a graduate of West Point and Stanford Business School. He's worked at Procter & Gamble, Boston Consulting Group, and CitySearch, and was thirty-eight when he became CEO of the Active Network, which runs websites that support sporting events nationally and locally. He's also a triathlete and mountain-bike racer to boot.

Alberga is a person who knows how to push his edge. When it comes to picking and choosing opportunities, he says, "At each new job, whatever presented itself—and lots of things did that I didn't pursue—it's always been something where I thought I could learn a ton. I never made decisions based on economics. I figured if I were in a growing area and doing good things, the money would be there. And that's worked out. But the driver always is, will I learn a ton and have fun and work with good people?"

> "I never made decisions based on economics. I figured if I were in a growing area and doing good things, the money would be there."

EXTREME JOB-INTERVIEWING SKILLS. ▸ Consider the following questions to be a starting point for researching any potential job and prepping for an interview. Job interviews become more complex the further you get in your career, but it's never too soon to take a kick-ass approach to the interviewing process.

But watch out all you Type-As: The job interview is also a situation where being extremely goal-oriented and competitive can work against you. That attitude can lead you to focus entirely on giving the "right" answers and "winning" the job. But you can end up neglecting the equally important task of finding out whether you actually *want* the job.

A *winning* candidate walks into a job interview already knowing what skills and experience the employer wants, and knows why it's looking for those particular things (in other words, what will the person they hire be asked to accomplish with his skill set?). He also knows the company's history, its products, what phase of life it's in (is it growing, trying to reinvigorate itself, in turnaround mode, or fighting off tough new competitors?), what major issues the company is facing, and what solutions his new boss will want him to bring to the table. That's called being prepared.

Once you have those basics down, you can make the interview about two things: helping the interviewer understand and appreciate how your skills and experience fit the job, and learning about the company culture and work environment. You should walk out of an interview with a good feel for how well the place would suit you. You should have some sense of what the person you talked to would be like to work for, if he or she was your potential boss, and what the job would add to your professional portfolio. Will there be plenty of opportunities to surf big waves, or just a better paycheck and a more impressive title?

Before walking into that interview, set some goals that will help you shape the meeting instead of just reacting to the people you meet. Ask yourself the following questions:

1. In general, what do you want to accomplish in this interview?

2. What are the three things you most want the interviewer(s) to know about you?

3. What do you still need to know about the opportunity under discussion?

4. What are three things you want to know about the boss, the department, and the company?

Once you're clear about what information you still need to know and the general issues you want to talk about, you can formulate more detailed questions for the interviewer and brainstorm ways to fit specific ideas you want to communicate during the conversation.

Tough questions and how to ask them

Sometimes the information you're most interested in is tricky to broach in an interview. How satisfied are the employees? What kind of boss will someone be? Does the CEO fully support the department's work? These issues are tough to bring up but necessary before you commit to a new job. Phrasing questions in creative ways can make them easier to pose, as can prefacing a tough question with a phrase like "Let me play devil's advocate for a minute."

Consider asking the following hard-hitting but valuable questions at your next interview. If they seem too aggressive for a first interview, ask them during a follow-up conversation, when it's clear that both you and the company are seriously interested in each other:

104

▌▌ Who has succeeded in this job previously, and what do you think made them effective? Where are they now?

▌▌ If you think about the people that you've worked best with over the course of your career, what do you think they have in common?

▌▌ How would others in this division/department/ group describe your management style?

▌▌ If I stood by the front door of the office at the end of the day, what would I see? (This is a polite way to get the following information: Would I see no one leaving because everyone works late? Would I see everyone leaving alone or groups heading off to play softball? Would I see stress or satisfaction on people's faces?)

▌▌ If you could change one thing about this company/ department/group, what would it be?

▌▌ Who would you recommend that I talk to in this group to get a more complete picture of the culture here and the issues you're facing as a group?

105

Five ways to wipe out—and how to avoid them

Extremely smart, talented, and successful people blow interviews all the time. Here are some interviewing blunders that could knock you out of the running:

Deal Breaker	Strategy
You're too hung up on titles.	As long as the title reflects the work you'll be doing, consider focusing on the opportunities the job will offer instead of what your business card says.
You're a self-promoter, but it's not clear whether you're a team player.	If a project was obviously a team effort, talk about what the team accomplished and then discuss your role—don't just talk about yourself.
You lack leadership skills.	Point out situations where you led by influence instead of direct authority, for example, by persuading people who don't report to you to support your mission, or by convincing a higher-up to pursue an idea he was reluctant to explore. (For more tips, see Chapter 5: Take Charge: Learn Leadership.)
You're short on social graces.	Don't blow off the receptionist who greets you when you walk in the door or the assistant who calls to schedule your interview. Do engage your interviewers as you're walking in or out of meetings with them, make eye contact, and don't forget to thank them for their time. And, please, turn off your cell phone and keep your PDA stowed away until you're out of the building.
You cave under stress.	Stay poised in the face of tough questions. If one seems especially harsh, ask the interviewer why she's asking or what her concerns are. It might prompt her to rephrase it or at least buy you some time.

108 || DANGER:
HAZARDOUS BOSS AHEAD

Philippe Bennett is an attorney whose eclectic life has taken him through several degrees (an A.B. in biochemistry from Harvard, an M.B.A. from Fordham University, and a J.D. from Hofstra University) and several firms, including Coudert Brothers LLP, on the path to being hired as a partner at Alston & Bird in New York. He's also an accomplished climber who's ascended Kilimanjaro and has his sights set on Mont Blanc, the highest peak in western Europe.

He recalls listening to a famous outdoorsman give a talk where he regaled the audience with tales of climbs gone wrong, cases where he'd narrowly escaped but others in his party weren't so lucky. Rather than being wowed, Bennett was put off. "I thought, I never want to go hiking with you. You always make it out okay, but your partners don't do so well," he says. "A career is just like climbing, there are times when you have to assess, Is this too unsafe?"

Just like that climber, some managers have a knack for self-preservation, and it can make them lousy at supporting the people who work for them. They're the men and women who are quick to pass blame and snatch credit. They're affronted if you aren't the workaholic they are. If underlings move on to better things, they view it as disloyalty rather than a credit to them. They often get their way by being loud and belligerent, rather than engaging and persuasive.

They're bad news. If you have an inkling that your potential boss might be a hazard to your own longevity, stay clear. After all, nobody bags a peak from under a pile of rocks. You don't want to be caught in an avalanche because your boss was too busy scrambling away to give you a heads-up.

FOLLOW UP, FOLLOW THROUGH, AND BAG THE JOB YOU REALLY WANT. ▶
So, let's say you had your first interview and you're feeling like this job might just be the perfect wave for you to ride to a new level of excellence. You've thoroughly scoped it out, checking the quality of the surf and identifying potential dangers. And you asked your interviewers the tough questions about the things that really matter to you and the answers checked out. In the days or weeks after that first interview, while you're waiting to hear back from your potential employer, you absolutely want to get in touch with anyone at the company that your interviewers suggested you to talk to.

Moreover, you want to call anyone you know who works or has worked for the company—or anyone you know who might know such people. Why? For starters, to make sure this opportunity has the potential to be as awesome and life-altering as it appears.

The fact is, some recruiters are up front about what a job entails and what sort of environment they offer because they want to hire someone who will thrive in the job and contribute to the company. But others aim to charm your socks off and say whatever will convince you to want the job. They're far less concerned with your personal growth and satisfaction than with filling the slot with someone impressive.

So, do yourself a favor and take your own reality check: Ask people who will be straight with you the same questions you asked your interviewers to make sure the answers sync. If they don't, your gut might start telling you to reconsider whether this is the perfect wave or a sure wipeout.

109

But if everything points to a pristine new stretch of ocean, with no hidden reefs or dangerous undertow, and awesome swells for the taking, then you want to be sure you get the offer, and that it's the sweetest deal you can negotiate for yourself.

How? You must have better follow-through than everyone else:

If an interviewer asks for follow-up information, or gives you a project to complete, get it to her sooner than she expects it.

If the recruiter refers you to others at the company, let him know that you got in touch and how those conversations helped you to better understand the company's issues and culture, and that you now have a better appreciation of how your experience fits the job.

If something great happens to you while you're waiting to hear back—you win an award, close a big deal, complete a class, get moved to a new assignment—make sure your interviewers know that you've become an even stronger candidate than you were when you met.

If the deadline for when the recruiter said you'd hear a decision comes and goes, follow up. If the bosses are torn between you and someone else, your aggressiveness, persistence, or full-on eagerness for the job (however they view it) might clinch it.

Once you have that offer, if you know you want it, negotiate your terms like you mean it.

Come to the table armed with knowledge of the company's salary range and other compensation for individuals at your level. It's also helpful to know what the industry's going rates are. And come prepared to ask for two or three perks that are important to you (they might include extra vacation time, job-hunting support for your spouse if you're relocating, permission to telecommute, flex time, or coverage of lifestyle expenses like a country club membership).

Rather than offending your future bosses, being an assertive, proactive (but reasonable) negotiator demonstrates that you know how to close a deal. It reassures them that you'll be equally tough but fair when you negotiate on the company's behalf. And it sends a clear message that you know what you're worth and that you stand up for yourself—a valuable precedent to set for those inevitable future discussions about your progress, raises, and promotions.

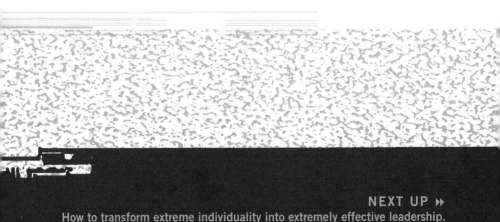

NEXT UP ▸▸
How to transform extreme individuality into extremely effective leadership.

END CHAPTER 4 ▪

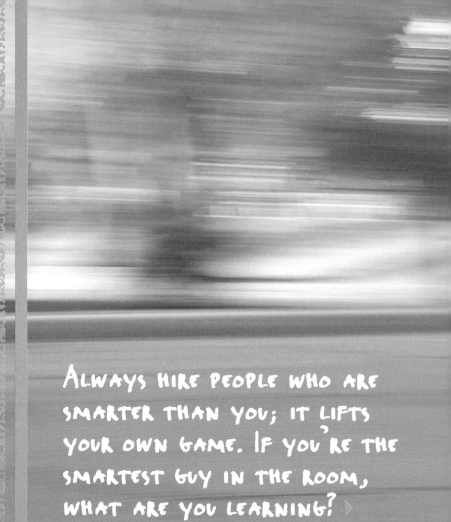

ALWAYS HIRE PEOPLE WHO ARE
SMARTER THAN YOU; IT LIFTS
YOUR OWN GAME. IF YOU'RE THE
SMARTEST GUY IN THE ROOM,
WHAT ARE YOU LEARNING?

—DAVE ALBERGA, CEO, THE ACTIVE NETWORK, AND TRIATHLETE

Chapter 5
Take Charge: Learn Leadership

STAND UP AND STAND OUT. ▸ We want strong team players.

It's the mantra of corporate America today, so ubiquitous it's a wonder everyone isn't walking around their cube farms in pinstripe uniforms and matching baseball hats.

But don't believe for a minute that surrendering your individuality to be entirely about The Team is a good thing for you or for your career. Whether you aspire to the pinnacles of corporate achievement or decide to forge a path all your own, to be extremely successful you have to take the ultimate risk of standing out and asserting yourself as a leader.

"Corporations talk all about teamwork, but I got a call from a headhunter just the other day who asked me, 'Who are the real standout people that I know. Who are the winners?'" says Neal Lenarsky, executive agent, whose Rolodex of

> # The "standout" individuals are the ones who are willing to step up and take charge of situations.

7,000 people, including quite a few standout performers, keeps him on the speed dials of top headhunters. He continues, "Look at someone like Rupert Murdoch. Strong individuals can get things done. That's why the recruiters look for those people."

The "standout" individuals are the ones who are willing to step up and take charge of situations and, yeah, get things done. So, chasing extreme success by being tirelessly *of* the team and *for* the team is like trying to snowboard in slush. You get too bogged down to gain any speed or momentum and you go nowhere.

But you can't be relentlessly for and about *yourself* either. Self-centered people alienate others, and it's hard to lead coworkers who are committed to avoiding you. As the recruiter Steve Mader observes, "Bad leaders hire in their own image. Good leaders hire alter egos who can play to their strengths and weaknesses."

Translating the individuality of an extreme athlete into extreme leadership in business means learning how to work *with* the team and be *for* the team while standing apart *from* the team.

Kinetic Leadership

Team members step up to lead at the things they're best at.

Project 1

Project 2

● Project Leader
● Team Member

Project 3

A NEW MODEL: KINETIC LEADERSHIP. ▸ For a lesson in teamwork and leadership, consider one of the few extreme sports that relies heavily on group work: adventure racing. An intense group expedition that spans a duration of anywhere from a few hours to ten days, adventure racing is a combination of two or more extreme sports—from cross-country running, paddling, and mountain biking to orienteering, navigation, and climbing skills. Members of these teams are often extremely accomplished at solo sports like endurance biking, kayaking, mountain climbing, and long-distance running. They're generally aggressive, competitive, and confident, and used to standing on their own very successfully. So, it took some time for Robyn Benincasa, a former Ironman triathlete herself, to find an adventure-racing group that could work together as a true team.

"Many people have tried to take athletic studs and incorporate them into a team and it never works," she says. Instead of the best athletes, she began looking for the best chemistry. "I want them to be trained, but I want them to be good people."

Her team strives for what she calls kinetic leadership, where "everyone on the team can stand out and lead at the thing they're best at, or in the circumstances where they're strongest." She says, "We appreciate that leadership is not about serving yourself but spreading your arms to bring the team along with you. We appreciate that the group's outcomes are bigger than our individual strengths.

Following this model, Benincasa has succeeded in pulling together a team that's won or placed in the biggest races. She now teaches what she's learned about leadership and teamwork to corporate audiences.

119

Back at the office, a kinetic leader is good at:

Advocating for what is good for your group (and, by association, good for you), instead of simply advocating for yourself.

Giving the people under you opportunities to exhibit their strengths and look good to those above you (in a way that reflects well on you).

Seeking feedback from others who have skills or experience you lack, instead of feeling threatened by them.

120

Soliciting and listening to input from people who are effected by the decisions you make, so they feel involved in rather than put-upon by those decisions.

YOU'RE IN CHARGE NOW: HOW TO LEAD FROM ABOVE. ▶ It's easier to stand up and take control if you've actually been put in charge of a team or a project. But to succeed in that role, to gain the big air that will get you to the next level, you have to win the support of your team; you can't just assume you already have it.

Chris Flint, another adventure racer and a senior vice president at Securities America in Omaha, Nebraska, is an example of a good team leader. He strives to create "a collaborative web" among the people who work for him. "You take the approach that we can all be successful together. Then you develop people to be committed to each other's success and you empower them."

Flint, who was in his early thirties when he was charged with developing new business for his company, readily shares information and constructive feedback with his peers and bosses, and he actively encourages his team to follow his lead.

For example, he notes, "I wanted to double the size of my sales team in the next twelve months and create regional vice presidents to manage those people. Before doing it, I got on the phone with one of my best sales guys to talk about the problems and opportunities that it would create for them."

121

Flint works to create an "employee-centric" workplace, "where people have the opportunity to present ideas," because he appreciates that this openness is what allowed him to move very quickly into leadership roles at the firm. It also makes it easier for him to continue producing impressive results as he climbs higher within the company and takes on more responsibility.

"Information-sharing is power," he explains. "We can make decisions very quickly and without a lot of noise here," because everyone is confident they know everything they need to about an issue, and they don't worry about someone's hidden agenda tripping them up later.

In contrast, he says, the old-school idea that "the more information I keep to myself, the more powerful I personally am," just undermines and stalls decision making. In an Internet-based global financial industry, that would prevent his group—and the company—from responding with due speed when opportunities or problems arise.

INFO
SHARING
=
POWER

STILL PART OF THE PACK? HOW TO LEAD FROM BELOW. ▶ Until you've worked your way into the CEO's office or launched your own business, there will always be someone above you. Knowing how to demonstrate your leadership skills to your boss, or your boss's boss, is a skill all by itself.

If you're still part of the pack (not in charge of it), then proving you're a leader is about being that strong individual who is willing to stand out, take risks, and put him- or herself on the line. For example, "I had access to decision makers from the days when I was a trader, and I was proactive in making sure I got my ideas out there," says Flint. "A lot of it is being able to offer critical assessment of your marketplace and organization. Then offering solutions and showing you can carry them out to effect change."

Frank Karbe, the investment-banker-turned-CFO, also set himself apart by spying opportunities to show off and then making sure he used his best moves to nail them. "At one point the market was booming and Goldman Sachs was always understaffed, so as a junior staffer I was sent out to client meetings that were usually run by more senior people," he recalls. "When it happened, I saw some people shy away, but I thought, *This* is an opportunity. Yeah, there's some risk, but if an opportunity presents itself, this is what makes your career."

Karbe recalls being at Goldman Sachs for less than a year when the head of his office asked him to prepare a last-minute presentation to a board of directors. Since this executive was somewhat of a celebrity in the German business world, Karbe was psyched to work with him. The young investment banker burned the midnight oil and got the presentation done just in time. "I handed him the books and thought I would sit back and watch this legendary guy at work," he says. Instead, the boss announced that Karbe would give the presentation.

Rather than getting psyched out, "I sat up and thought, 'Wow, this is my chance to define what he thinks of me'." He gathered his thoughts and did the presentation well enough to earn a compliment from the chairman of the company he was presenting to.

Talk about sticking your landing after a 450-degree spin...

123

Find a boss who shares your leadership style—otherwise you're pulling your best tricks for people who don't have the capacity to be impressed.

If you are literally a middle manager, with people both above and below you, then you prove your leadership cred by advocating for your team and proving you can motivate them to deliver major results.

Benjamin Wagner has gotten ahead at MTV News by making sure the websites and digital content he's responsible for look awesome and by always delivering the goods. But at every turn, he makes sure his team and his media get the attention and resources they need to perform to their peak capacity, too.

"I do advocate for my team's capabilities," he says. "And I do a lot more proselytizing for the digital [component]. I said three times in a meeting today, 'Don't forget we have to do digital and broadband and the web.'"

His willingness to step up for his team and promote their work paves the way for him to successfully advocate for himself as well. "I told my boss I want to be an executive producer by a certain date, and fundamentally it happened," the marathoner says. "But first I had to demonstrate to myself and my boss what I could do. It boiled down to patience and persistence."

Finally, find a boss who shares your leadership style—otherwise you're pulling your best tricks for people who don't have the capacity to be impressed. "If you want to be able to say, 'The team's success is my success,' you have to make sure the person evaluating you values that; it flows downward," Benincasa notes.

Extreme Inspiration

A successful balancing act

Jens Beck, *a triathlete and mountain runner, is a vice president at SKW/Eskimos, a construction company that's part of a larger oil-services company in Alaska. A big part of his job is balancing his role as a leader within his unit with his obligation to be a team player for the larger company. "You have to set priorities and pick your battles," he says. "Sometimes you can toe the corporate line or be respected internally, but you can't do both. I've chosen to be respected internally."*

The youthful thirty-something describes the leadership style of his boss, whom he calls a role model, in similar terms: "He has a lot of integrity. He stands for what is right, and not what will get him the most money or the next promotion."

Not everyone at Beck's sprawling conglomerate approaches teamwork and leadership the same way, which he finds frustrating. But his direct supervisor shares his management style, so he values his work and makes sure that others do, too.

At one point during a recent reorganization, Beck began scouting for a new job. He quickly got an attractive offer to be the CFO elsewhere, but his boss told the execs at the parent company about the offer and played a role in negotiating a counteroffer. "He encouraged me to look around, and helped me to think about whether I would stay," says Beck. "But knowing [the higher-level execs] wanted me to stay was nice." And so it was that Jens Beck, acknowledged and respected in his workplace, decided that staying onboard was the best possible choice.

A few words of caution:
How to alienate people in five easy steps

126

Entertainment-industry exec Matt Jacobson learned as much from the one lousy boss he survived as from the several good ones he thrived under. Of the not-so-cool situation, he recalls, "He wanted you accessible twenty-four/seven, but he was never around. Everything good that happened was because of him and everything bad was because of you. I realized quickly that it's a pretty crappy way to run your life."

Surefire ways to become the centerpiece of somebody else's worst-boss story:

1. **Make all decisions unilaterally without a reality check from the people who have to live with them.**

2. **Be quick to pass blame for team missteps and to claim credit for team success.**

3. **Routinely promise to support, help, or advise others, knowing that you won't follow through. (This will quickly get you voted "most disingenuous.")**

4. **Motivate people by being harsh, critical, and bullying instead of mellow, constructive, and engaging.**

5. **Hoard information that would be beneficial to your whole team so that you can use it later to undermine a colleague or inflate your own importance.**

Extreme Inspiration

Scaling the leadership learning curve

A person who spent six years living in a Volkswagen van crisscrossing the country to rock-climb and who now spends hours contemplating boulders, trying to come up with the best way to scale them, is probably a person who values his solitude. And Concept2's **Bill Patton,** *who has done all of those things and more, is the first to admit he's not a great people person.*

128

But to be a director of anything at a small but fast-growing company requires the ability to engage people and get stellar results out of them. And to be in charge of marketing, as he is, means knowing how to communicate effectively and bring people together. Patton describes himself as "the connector" between several parts of his company.

So, how did this loner turn himself into a leader? "This has been and continues to be a struggle for me," he says. "I have to remind myself to get up and walk around and talk to people face to face; to listen, interact, and be patient. The challenge was to find a company that would allow someone like myself (a quiet thinker as opposed to a loud alpha male–type leader) to have an impact on strategic direction," he explains.

As he's progressed in his career and become more confident in the value of the things he's extremely good at, he's become less threatened by people who come by strong people skills more naturally. "I used to be very defensive about not being good at that. But I've come to realize that the people who have that ability—it's a real talent," he says. "And I realize that I'm better, my group is better, and the company is better if I take advantage of others' people skills."

Now, he says, "I surround myself with people who do have social skills, then rely on them to blunt my sometimes abrupt style." That frees him up for the work that makes use of "the intellectual and strategic skills" that set him apart from the pack.

The Connector

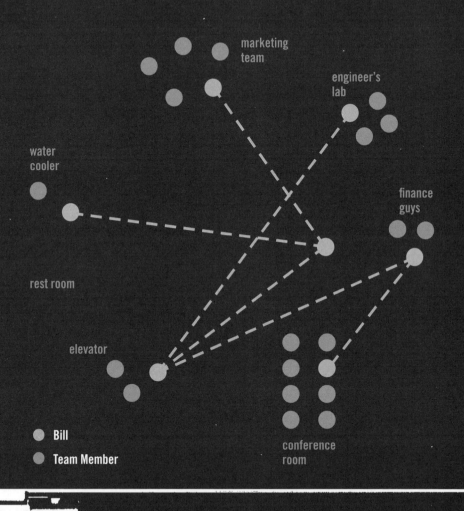

marketing
team

engineer's
lab

water
cooler

finance
guys

rest room

elevator

● Bill

● Team Member

conference
room

NEXT UP ▸▸
Do you have what it takes to go out on your own?

END CHAPTER 5 ■

In skydiving or business or any endeavor, if something is worth doing you're gonna run up against yourself—a wall or your comfort zone. Pushing yourself beyond that, you might get hurt—or you might be able to handle it.

—David Becker, competitive skydiver and entrepreneur

Chapter **6**

Are You Ready to
Go Out on Your Own?

TAKING EXTREME TO THE EXTREME. ▶ A refresher: Being extreme means pushing aside fear, accepting risk, and taking control of your career. You hold out for the opportunities that truly engage and excite you, and push your edge further and further out, so that you can achieve more than you ever thought was possible.

For some of you, working for yourself may be the extreme far end of the extreme spectrum. You start your own company, become a free agent, or even sign on to help launch someone else's company because you're ready to be in a situation where the only things holding you back are your own fears, lack of ability, or limited imagination. You know that if you conquer those things, your opportunities for growth, achievement, and wealth are limitless. You want a situation where you can work an edge that's too far out to even see.

Extreme Career Spectrum

Extreme Far End

Entrepreneur

Free Agent

Hired Gun

Intrapreneur

Employee

● You are where?

The characteristics that allow a person to succeed at extreme sports or an extreme career—

FOCUS

ANALYTICAL PROWESS

PSYCHOLOGICAL STAMINA

INDIVIDUALITY

UNDERSTANDING AND ACCEPTANCE OF RISK

—are also crucial to entrepreneurs. Here's how a person who works for him- or herself applies these keys qualities:

FOCUS is being clear on what you want to do and where you want to go with your business. Without it, you can't tell a compelling story about your business, and you won't convince your partners, employees, investors, and customers to take a leap of faith and support you.

Alain Chuard, the ex–Wall Streeter, recalls struggling to translate his vague idea of offering snowboarding vacations for grown-ups into a well-defined business plan to provide instructional tours in a range of settings around the world. "By talking to people and reading books, we developed a strong vision that can be applied to sports and to other lines of travel, too," he says. Having this focus "gives our employees a sense of where we're going. It's the holy grail we're all trying to get to."

ANALYTICAL PROWESS is the ability to think your way through tough and complex problems that you've never faced before, that perhaps no one has, and do so on your own steam.

Bill Patton, the veteran climber and boulderer in Vermont, says that he likes working for a small company and "being close to the fire" because he relishes the intellectual challenge. "I know the joy of ascending a tough problem." And he's ready for all the challenges—in work and in play—that might come his way. "I'm always on the lookout for them," he says.

When it comes to both bouldering (where people come up with ways to traverse the surfaces of giant rocks, Spider-Man–style), and working for a start-up, he says, "It takes a particular kind of intellect to be able to see a problem that no one else has seen before. You have to decide if it can't be solved; if it can, but it's too hard for you; or if you can do it if you try really, really hard."

PSYCHOLOGICAL STAMINA is the ability to zone out the problems, flux, and chaos that come with getting a new business off the ground so that you can keep your focus locked on your big-picture goals and immediate priorities.

Soon after Chuard launched Access Adventure Travel, he found himself speeding along a learning curve as steep as the walls of a half-pipe. "I had to learn how to recruit people to work for us without a lot of resources. I had to learn

how to market to potential clients. I had to learn strategic thinking and techno-logical ways to make the business more efficient." And he had to corral those wide-ranging efforts around the bigger goal of building a kick-ass portfolio of education-centric tours.

But the real test of his fortitude was his timing. He launched the company in July 2001 and almost immediately ran up against 9/11, the recession, and the Iraq War. While pushing himself to learn and grow fast, he also had to find ways to move his business forward in a tough economic climate. "I had to be the one to stay positive and motivate people. I had to say everything makes sense: We have a strong vision and a good concept and we just have to stick to it." Some-times the extreme entrepreneur or leader has to be an extreme cheerleader.

INDIVIDUALITY is personified by Rick Alden, founder of Skullcandy and maker of the "mind-blowing, punk rock consumer electronic products" that are his signature. This entrepreneur is a guy who knows beyond a shadow of a doubt who he is and what drives him.

137

You need Alden's crystal clear sense of self to walk away from a traditional company because there are experiences you want that your present employer just can't offer. And you need his confidence to trust that you can live without a big company's cash, prestige, and staff because you have everything you need to succeed somewhere deep inside you.

UNDERSTANDING AND ACCEPTANCE OF RISK is one of the most impor-tant keys to your extreme lifestyle. Entrepreneurs have a reputation for being risk-seeking daredevils who are bored if they aren't taking chances that make the rest of us gape (think Richard Branson). But the most successful entrepreneurs don't necessarily see themselves as more risk-tolerant than the average person.

"I'm just different in what I view as risky," says Dave Alberga, who has been part of the founding team for three start-ups, including the Active Network. "I don't view putting myself in a less stable career position as risky. It's just more exciting and interesting than what I could be spending my time doing."

The fact that something is scary isn't a reason not to do it (if you think it is, you're reading the wrong book).

He's well aware that the stakes are serious—"My business might fail and I might be out of the job."—but his philosophy is actually quite positive. "I don't perceive unemployment as that risky," he says. "I'd be much more scared of waking up and realizing that I'm doing something I don't like, and that I've wasted years working for people who don't care about me and not contributing to the greater good."

What you view as risky and how much risk you can handle has everything to do with what makes you feel safe and secure and what makes you feel vulnerable.

Remember Rick Alden's descriptions of his experiences working for a large company versus working for himself. Like Alberga, Alden doesn't see failure as something inherently bad or insurmountable, so he's not afraid of it. However, lack of control over his work and his ability to earn a living makes him feel vulnerable. So to him, working for a big corporation, where layoffs can descend out of the blue to leave you with no job and no income, presents a bigger risk than starting a business.

That's not to say there isn't risk in going out on your own. There is. You're putting tangible things on the line—the livelihood of anyone you hire, for example, and the money (yours, your partners', your family's, your investors') that you control. Losing real money and putting real people out of real jobs are possible consequences that should be taken seriously. To start a business, you have to be able to fully appreciate potential downsides, too.

If that sounds scary, that's okay. The fact that something is scary isn't a reason not to do it (if you think it is, you're reading the wrong book). There's a woman in New Zealand, Emma Hawke, who's a champion rock climber and is afraid of heights. It seems completely counterintuitive, but it's not that unusual. She explained in an interview with a local newspaper, "You're so focused on what you want to achieve that sometimes you do things that aren't normal for you."

Whether it's scaling a rock wall, breaking away from a job that's absurdly limiting, or building a new venture from the ground up, the need to accomplish can be strong enough to push aside your anxiety about what could go wrong. Learning to manage your vulnerabilities and live with your fears becomes just another aspect of pushing your edge.

139

1. **The opportunity they want most doesn't exist, so they go create it for themselves. (Remember Neal Lenarsky, who invented the job of executive agent.)**

2. **They have an idea for a new product or service that's so compelling, they just have to find out if it will work.**

3. **The old way of working doesn't work for them. They believe there has to be a better way—and are determined to figure it out.**

4. **They believe they work too hard to settle for just a salary. If they're going to commit unlimited hours and effort to their work, they want the potential for unlimited profits.**

5. **They've been burned by big-company politics, disloyalty, and bureaucracy, and don't want to have to rely on an employer ever again.**

If you have the urge to strap on a parachute and skydive into entrepreneurship but you're not sure you have the nerve to step out of a nice, safe plane into the open air, just keep in mind that most traditional companies offer the illusion of security, not the real thing. Between 1996 and 2004, the U.S. averaged more than 1.8 million layoffs a year. Even in 1999, the height of the "New Economy" boom, some 1.6 million people lost their jobs overnight through mass layoffs.

The fact is, you aren't giving up that much safety or stability by jumping—your parachute may even prove more reliable than that big old jet plane. So why not take the leap and try that new venture that's gonna blow your mind and let you find out what you're really made of?

Three entrepreneurial models

You may envision an entrepreneur as someone who's willing to bet their retirement fund on their own vision. But there's more than one way to pursue the entrepreneurial life. Which one is right for you? That depends on your goals and motivations. Consider these three basic models and you'll recognize the best fit for you when the time is right. **Or, to consider whether *intra*preneurship might be right for you, see page 146.** ▶▶

Find out what you're really made of.

DEVELOP THAT NEW PRODUCT OR SERVICE THAT'S BEEN GNAWING AWAY AT YOU.

FIND A NEW WAY OF WORKING THAT MAKES YOU MORE SATISFIED AND PUMPED THAN THE 9-TO-5 (OR 9-TO-9!) GRIND.

WORK YOUR ASS
OFF FOR SOMETHING
THAT'S VITALLY
IMPORTANT TO YOU,
INSTEAD OF WORKING
FOR SOMETHING THAT 143
SOMEONE ELSE HAS
DECIDED IS IMPORTANT.

Three Entrepreneurial Models

	The creator
What you do	Take an idea you believe in and build a company around it from scratch.
What's on the line	Whatever money you or other people invest; your reputation and ego; other people's jobs.
What you have to be good at	Initially, everything. Later on, knowing what you're actually good at so you can hire people who are good at the other things.
Cash-flow situation	Early on, you pay everyone else and plunge what's left into growing the business. Eventually, if the business is successful, you can pay yourself a hefty salary and consider cashing in on an IPO or sale.
The end goal	Grow the company until it can run on its own momentum rather than on your sheer willpower. That way, it can continue to speed along if you sell it, retire, or otherwise step aside.
The hard part	Remaining focused and motivated when there's no guarantee of money or established structure, and you have to find your own way through problems, changing circumstances, and everyday chaos.
What you stand to gain	Best-case scenario: fame and fortune. At the very least, total control over your destiny and the chance to create something.
Extreme role models	Martha Stewart, Amazon.com's Jeff Bezos, Starbucks's Howard Schultz

The hired gun	The free agent
Take someone else's idea and build a company around it.	Hire out your skills as you define them. Lecture, write, teach, invest.
Someone else's baby, other people's jobs, other people's money, your credibility.	As much money as you spend on your office set-up and invest in business ventures; your reputation and employability.
Taking someone else's idea and owning it so you can grow the company like mad; creating structure where there isn't any; motivating people to achieve a lot, often on a shoestring budget.	Convincing people they need what you've got; working entirely on your own and by yourself; managing the other free agents that you hire when business is really good.
You'll probably have a salary, but you may also be asked to pass up some cash now for shares of stock or potential profit-sharing later.	When you stop working, the money stops flowing.
To get the company to a fixed point, such as the next round of venture capital, an IPO, or sale, or a certain level of revenue.	Become the go-to person that everyone thinks of first for challenging projects. Do it for as long as you think it's awesome, or until even more compelling work comes your way.
Trying to achieve big air with limited resources. Keeping all the stakehold-ers—employees, investors, founders, and yourself—happy.	Constantly selling yourself and staying self-motivated and self-disciplined.
Best-case scenario: fame and fortune. At the very least, almost total control over your destiny and the chance to create something lasting.	Best-case scenario: As much money as you're willing to work for and ample personal freedom. At the very least, the ability to say no when you want to.
eBay's Meg Whitman, Google's Eric Schmidt	Tom Peters, Ram Charon, William Bridges

ARE YOU AN INTRAPRENEUR? ▶ Traditional companies that reward innovation, independence, and entrepreneurship still exist—here and there. Using your extreme-career skills to be an intrapreneur can offer the best of both worlds: Major resources *and* plenty of room to work your edge and grab that big air.

Consider how two extreme executives have done just that:

Following a stint developing new-media projects for News Corp., **Matt Jacobson** moved to Broadcom, where he created an extreme sports television show called *Bluetorch*, along with other entertainment projects. He hadn't been there long when Quiksilver, a maker of clothing and gear for snowboarding and surfing, invited him to produce a television show that they could use to promote their products.

"They wanted me to do another *Bluetorch*, but I saw a bigger play," and he asked for six months to write a business plan, he recalls. He came back with a vision to partner with a range of media outlets to produce books, movies, and television shows that would be profitable projects in their own right, and would promote surfing and snowboarding lifestyles without explicitly pushing Quiksilver products. "Size is the opposite of cool in youth. They don't react to something that's that obvious," he says. But if you showcase a lifestyle and a look, he reasoned, you generate interest and create a tide that lifts all boats, including yours.

Jacobson earned the opportunity to start up Quiksilver Entertainment, which produced a show about surfer girls for MTV, a documentary called *Riding Giants*, which played at the Sundance Film Festival, and a book series for pre-teen girls, among other hip projects.

Despite spending most of his career at large, public companies, Jacobson says, "I like being able to create something that wasn't there." He's been focused, determined, and smart about creating opportunities where he can do just that. "I've been aggressively entrepreneurial," he notes.

146

Karl Quist cut his business teeth at the elite consulting firm McKinsey & Co., but after a few years of telling CEOs how to run their businesses, he wanted to run something himself.

An avid windsurfer since he was a kid, Quist is experienced at working out complicated problems, like how to keep your balance on your board while judging wind and managing your sail. "I had to figure a lot of things out for myself because there was no one to ask." Not surprisingly, as an adult, he was more interested in running a small, agile company than a big lumbering one.

He sought out a business development job and found his ideal opportunity with Landmark Communications, a media company in Virginia. He launched a handful of projects related to the company's newspaper and television properties, all the while keeping his eye out for a business he'd want to run. Eventually, Quist's bosses asked him to come up with a project that would leverage the Internet and streaming media.

Despite combing the far reaches of his cable box, he'd always had a hard time finding windsurfing programs on television, or DVDs at the video store. That made him believe that streaming video could be an inexpensive way to broadcast sports-related programming to small, hard-core audiences. He put together a business plan for TotalVid—a company that offers instructional and entertaining videos related to niche activities like wakeboarding, inline skating, martial arts, and windsurfing. And much, much more.

"Usually I'd come up with ideas and someone else executed. But this one I wanted to do," Quist says. "This was an opportunity to build something from scratch, which is something that not everyone gets to do. No one knows what the future holds [for broadband content] because the business isn't well defined yet; we're in the middle of doing that."

Like many extreme athletes in the business world, he enjoys being kept on his toes. "There are challenges every day, like trying to figure out what different technology developments mean for our business." He concludes, "It's got a lot of what drew me to windsurfing [in the first place]."

GET YOUR BUSINESS INTO COMPETITION-READY CONDITION. ▸ It goes without saying that extreme athletes who want to compete (and win) in the biggest games—the Ironman for triathletes, the Olympics for snowboarders, the Raid World Championship for adventure racers, to name a few—have a plan for getting there. They know what muscles they need to develop and what skills they need to build, and they plot out the training schedules they need to keep to meet those goals, with milestones to track their progress.

If you're going to build a company, you need to have a training plan, too. It should state your significant goals, like completing a prototype, getting a product to market, hitting certain sales or revenue targets, or signing up clients of a certain size. And your training plan must also lay out what you have to do to achieve these goals—milestones along the way that will keep you focused and motivated.

Consider David Becker's training plan, then consider your own. ▸

Extreme Inspiration
Training to win

Before **David Becker** became president of Philippe Becker Design, a branding and packaging firm he founded with his brother, he spent several years as a competitive formation skydiver. Despite its reputation as a sport for renegades with a kamikaze streak, getting to a level where you can win national titles (his team did, twice) takes an extreme amount of discipline and a surprisingly long-term view. "I have an MBA from a good school and I probably learned as much from this experience as I did from business school," he says.

149

He was given a skydiving jump for his twenty-fifth birthday, doubted he would like it, but saw it as a dare and did it anyway. "It was a revelation to me. I thought I'm never gonna not do this. And then I really got into it."

He and his wife and another couple organized a formation skydiving team and hired an alumnus of the elite U.S. Army Golden Knights parachute team to coach them. "He was very disciplined. He had a three-year plan for us. In the first year you'll get good at this and in the second year, this, and in the third year you can open it up and put it all together," Becker recalls. "It was a new approach to me, to learn these pods of information really well and then line them up one on top of the other. It's a methodology that's worked very well for me in business."

When he abandoned a corporate career to work with his brother in 2001, he formulated a similar multi-year training plan. "Our approach was not about trying to hoard the riches and scoop everything in our direction all at once. It was more to build the framework right," he explains.

The plan: "We were going to eat dirt for three years. We'd charge less than we could to get big clients and blow them away. Then plow all the money back into the business. It was: Get credible for the first three years, and then leverage that."

They carefully cultivated relationships with the clients his brother could bring in from networking and from his previous work experience—even if it meant taking small projects to get their foot in the door. They joined the Chamber of Commerce and took on high-profile pro bono work. And once they had a track record, they hired a public relations person to make sure word got out about them. "Our business is so much about reputation. So when we've had success, we'll talk about it. We want to create an aura of can-do that people want to be a part of."

The firm now boasts a 96-percent retention rate and was named one of the fastest growing private companies in San Francisco in 2005, which suggests that their "can-do aura" is expanding into a parachute that will keep them aloft for a while.

150

The Plan

Significant Goals

How will you get there (the training)?

Milestones
3 months:

6 months:

9 months:

1 year:

2 years:

3 years:

Get Yourself a Sponsor

It's usually pretty obvious what your sponsor can do for you, but a strong sustaining relationship is a two-way street. Figure out what opportunities you can offer your sponsor, too.

Sponsor   **You**

Opportunities

YOU NEED A SPONSOR. HERE'S HOW TO GET ONE. ▶ Going out on your own isn't quite going solo, because once you're on your own, relationships will be more important than they've ever been to you. You need people who can give you moral support, advice, clients, references, and money. You'll have to rely heavily on your ability to persuade people you know to introduce you to people they know.

Among those myriad relationships, what you need most are people who are willing to be your sponsors. As is the case with extreme athletes, entrepreneurs' sponsors provide more than money. They lend advice, credibility, contacts, and visibility that you can parlay into opportunities. (Remember, Robyn Benincasa launched her corporate consulting business when she made a connection at an appearance for her sponsor.)

Sponsors obviously include the venture capitalists and angels who invest cold hard cash in you, but they can also be your customers, vendors, former employers, colleagues, and anyone else in your circle who can boost your credibility or visibility. The sponsorship might be formal or informal, lasting or a one-time event. And money might not even be a part of the deal.

After working as an executive recruiter for eight years and graduating from a boutique firm to industry giant Heidrick & Struggles, Matthew Schwartz wanted to go out on his own. "I thought, instead of working for a firm and keeping fifty percent of what I bring in, why not work myself and keep eighty percent?" he says.

He was up-front with his bosses about his plans and worked to maintain relationships with his former colleagues at the firm after he left. Now a good chunk of his business comes through Heidrick & Struggles referrals. "I can make money on smaller assignments they won't take on, so they send things my way," Schwartz explains.

He doesn't have any formal arrangement with the firm but these referrals are an informal endorsement. The result: His former employer is a sponsor who gives him business as well as credibility he can use to generate other clients. "They've been crucial," he says.

153

Think you don't happen to know anyone who can provide the kind of sponsorship you need? Then it's time to start cultivating the relationships that can help you find and connect with people who can help you.

When Trey Gregory was on the free-skiing circuit and needed a sponsor, he quickly learned that skiing well was only part of what he needed to do to win one. Equipment makers also wanted photogenic skiers who could catch the attention of photographers and wind up pictured (with the sponsor's gear) in ski magazines and on websites. So he cultivated relationships with local photographers and built a portfolio of images of himself in action.

Then he parlayed a relationship with a fellow ski instructor to get into a trade show that amateurs don't normally have access to, so he could get his portfolio in front of ski-company people. "She introduced me to a rep she knew. I sat down with him and walked away with a local sponsorship. I was walking on air," he recalls. In exchange for skis and other gear, he would promote the company on the local circuit he skied.

Gregory appreciated his connections, and he understood that you can't walk up to a sponsor empty-handed. He came prepared to offer something of value to them—this is something every extreme entrepreneur must understand.

It's usually pretty obvious what your sponsor can do for you, but a strong, sustaining relationship is a two-way street. If you want support, be prepared to tell your potential sponsor what you can do for him.

Adventure racer Robyn Benincasa and her team have sponsorship deals with Merrell, the outdoor-shoe company, and Zanfel Laboratories, as well as with PowerBar and a handful of equipment companies. Racing is way too expensive to do without a sponsor (remember, each competition can involve as many as half a dozen sports). A sponsor provides essential gear and covers entry fees and other costs along the way.

"I think about who they're trying to reach and how I can use my connections to help them. And I present the team as consultants instead of athletes," Benincasa explains.

154

In addition to appearances to promote products, she's given presentations to one sponsor's employees in an effort to raise awareness about health and fitness. For another company, she used her relationships with race coordinators to get product information and samples into orientation packets for several events. She and her racing teammates have provided feedback on the usefulness and marketing of some products, and have even had a hand in designing others.

"You don't want to just be a billboard; there has to be something tangible in the business sense," she says.

What do you have to offer your own sponsors? It might be something overt or something subtle. Maybe you have relationships or expertise they can make use of. Maybe being associated with you raises their profile in a way that wouldn't otherwise be available to them.

For example, venture capitalists and angels aren't philanthropists; they're looking for opportunities to make a lot of money on a relatively inexpensive investment. What you bring to the table is that potential for growth.

Matthew Schwarz provides Heidrick & Struggles with a way to turn down business that isn't right for the firm while still providing a valuable connection to their customers.

You'll have to pay for the sponsorship in one way or another, so think about what currency you have to offer, then get out there and spend it wisely by cultivating relationships that will further your personal goals.

NEXT UP ▸▸
Get out of the office; improve your job skills while you're at it.

END CHAPTER 6 ■

WANT TO GET BETTER AT YOUR JOB?
THEN GET OUT OF THE OFFICE. ▶

Fast Forward

Chapter 7
Extreme Work, Extreme Play

PRACTICE AN EXTREME SPORT; FIND WORK-LIFE BALANCE. ▸ You might already be an extreme-sports junkie who hoards all your nonworking hours and vacation time to get out on the slopes, the swells, or the rocks for some serious, adrenaline-pumping adventure. Or maybe you're at the other end of the spectrum, and you think it sounds insane to pile a time-consuming, physically and mentally challenging sport (or several) on top of a time-intensive, demanding, and high-profile job. But most of the people interviewed for this book do just that.

Frank Karbe, who began training for an Ironman triathlon while CFO at Exelixis, would rise early for a pre-work run and then go swimming after late-night business dinners. When she was part of a slalom-racing team, Risa Shimoda would endure freezing early-morning paddling sessions, then drive to work with her kayak atop her car. As a second-year investment banker, Alain Chuard trained hard enough to qualify for the U.S. national half-pipe snowboarding championships.

But rather than distracting them from their hard-driving jobs and careers, the extreme sports help them to be better in their professional pursuits. If you're already addicted to snowboarding or long-distance running or skydiving, you probably agree with marathoner and media exec Benjamin Wagner: "The athleticism and job and personal life overlap to the point where it's hard to tell where one ends and one begins," he says. "And I get energy from being active. The more I do, the more energy I feel I have."

The fact is, having dual passions brings balance to lives where work could easily be all-consuming. Both the enthusiasts and the pros make a point of carving out time for their sports however they can. And slipping in an hour of lunchtime snowboarding or leaving promptly at 5:30 to catch a few waves or take a long bike ride gives them valuable personal space they use to chill out, reenergize, and gain a fresh perspective on things. Sound familiar? If not, read on.

"Training is the one time in the entire day when the phone isn't ringing, the BlackBerry isn't vibrating, and people aren't walking in. They can relax, let their minds go, and think deep thoughts," says Ted Kennedy, who founded CEO Challenge, a company that provides logistical support for executives who do marathons or triathlons. "A lot of executive triathletes say that if they have a problem they can't solve, they just take a long run and a solution will present itself along the way."

Moreover, by ripping into their sports with abandon, they've learned what it's like to have real passion for something. And they know what it means to commit to something bigger than themselves and to achieve in an awesome way as a result. Sarah Reinertsen, the first female amputee to finish the Ironman Triathlon World Championship in Kona, Hawaii, told a reporter, "Coming down that finishing chute is something I'll never forget. It's a high I certainly could get addicted to."

Whatever their work situation, they find a way to create space for their sporting passions. Why make that gargantuan effort? Because this passion fuels their extreme careers, and it can fuel yours, too. These achievers want to commit as much energy and intensity to their work as they do to the slopes or the waves or the racecourse, and they expect to get excitement, achievement, and deep satisfaction in return.

Additionally, these athletes use their sports to hone the traits and characteristics that have helped them to succeed in their careers—focus, risk tolerance, emotional stamina, individuality, and a knack for problem solving. Alain Chuard prepares mentally for business school exams, big meetings, and job interviews the same way he used to psych himself up for athletic competitions. David Becker used the same training strategy to build his design firm that he used to become a champion skydiver.

IF YOU WANT TO GET BETTER AT YOUR JOB, GET OUT OF THE OFFICE. ▶

Maybe you've already made the extreme sport–extreme career connection yourself. **161** If so, then we hope this book is fanning those flames. Or maybe you're an extreme-sports virgin, but you're tempted to rip, shred, and tear out in the open air.

Well, you ought to be. You *can* cultivate some of the extreme traits outlined in this book by way of other nonextreme life experiences, even through work itself. "Confidence comes from depth of experience. By going through things that were hard but turned out okay, you learn more about what you believe is possible," observes recruiter Steve Mader. "You might take that experience from mountain climbing or from a business situation where your prospects looked slim but you made it through."

But by getting out of the office and learning to snowboard or surf or rock-climb or free-ski, you battle burnout. You come back energized and better able to push aside distractions so you can pursue those things about your job and your career that excite you. And you get to put yourself in a new and unfamiliar environment, which is all by itself a way of pushing your edge.

And besides, work *is* work. Learning from play is a helluva lot more fun, isn't it?

IF YOU ALREADY
PRACTICE YOUR
EXTREME SPORT
OF CHOICE WITH
TOTAL PASSION,
FEEL FREE TO
SKIP AHEAD TO
PAGE 172. ▶▶▏

...but if you're contemplating your options, here are some things for you to consider. What your extreme-sport experience will be depends on a few factors:

Where do you live? How often do you travel?

How much free time do you have?

What is your physical condition?

How are you built?

What are you good at?

What are you interested in?

Do you want an episodic experience or an ongoing one?

If you have just a few hours a week to spare, you can head to a local indoor climbing wall to take lessons and practice rock-climbing. If you can spare fifteen to twenty hours a week (including weekends), from three months to a year, you can think about training for a marathon, long-distance bike ride, or even a triathlon.

For activities you might have to travel to try out, like outdoor climbing, kayaking, snowboarding, surfing, or mountain biking, a weekend is enough time for a crash course. After two or three days you won't be a master, but you'll know whether you want to become a regular weekend warrior.

Your sport might reflect the traits and skills you already have or those you want to develop.

If you can spare ten days to a couple of weeks, though, travel somewhere exotic and tackle real mountain climbing, or immerse yourself in snowboarding or surfing, or sign up at a kayaking school.

Or push your edge some other way that you find appealing. You can step out of your comfort zone and challenge your mind and your body by way of an adventure vacation—trekking in Patagonia or going on safari in Kenya—or by volunteering to build houses in rural America or a school in a developing country.

Your sport might reflect the traits and skills you already have or those you want to develop.

To some extent, any extreme sport will cultivate all the traits and skills discussed in this book. But each sport emphasizes one or two characteristics in particular. Skydiving, for example, has almost everything to do with determination and accepting and managing risk. Bouldering will teach you as much about concentration and problem solving as any advanced-math class could. And motocross requires major endurance and stamina, and—particularly if you like to finish the race in one piece—strong analytical skills.

You can choose to indulge your strongest skills and inclinations or to cultivate your weakest.

Where you hit your edge, and how far you need to push to get the hang of a sport and then master it, depends on you. You can choose to indulge your strongest skills and inclinations or to cultivate your weakest. You can benefit from either. Building your innate skills makes you even stronger. But going against your natural inclinations and pushing the edge that's foreign might teach you more about yourself and what you're capable of.

Bill Patton observes, "I know people who are risk-averse but who have decided they want to do something like learn to rock-climb. So they grit their teeth and overcome their fear and become good at that activity. These people who are risk-averse but struggle with it are often the best to climb with—they're cautious and they think things through."

CHOOSE THE SPORT, LEARN THE SKILLS, PUSH YOUR LIMITS: AN EXTREME-ADVENTURE SAMPLER. ▸ The following pages offer overviews of some sports to consider exploring if you really want to push your limits—both in and out of the workplace.

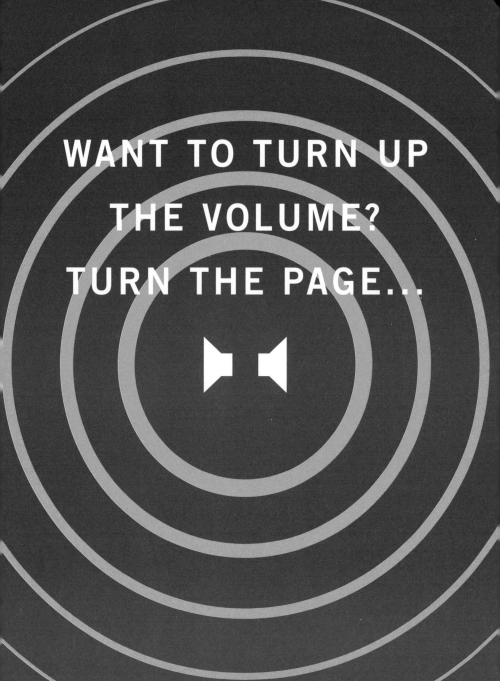

Extreme Determination

The sport: mountain climbing

How to start: day hikes where you can prime your muscles and lung capacity and practice some wall climbing and scrambling

What to aim for: multiday treks in the Rockies or Andes or Alps

Think even bigger: climb one of the Seven Summits

Resources:
www.ime-usa.com
www.alpineascents.com
www.emsclimb.com

Psychological Stamina and Extreme Endurance

The sport: triathlons

How to start: train for a sprint or "fun" race (a 200- to 500-yard swim, a 5- to 10-mile bike ride, and a 3- to 5-mile run)

What to aim for: a mid-distance run with tough terrain, like San Francisco's Escape from Alcatraz race

Think even bigger: your first Ironman

Resources:
www.usatriathlon.org
www.beginnertriathlete.com
www.ceochallenges.com

Analytical Prowess

The sport: rock climbing

How to start: an indoor climbing wall where you can take lessons

What to aim for: Ancient Art, a corkscrew-shaped tower in Moab, Utah, with climbs that are 5.8 and higher (on a scale of 5.0–5.13)

Think even bigger: Liberty Ridge, on Mount Rainier; training ground for anyone who aspires to expedition climbs

Resources:
www.rockclimbing.com
www.ime-usa.com
www.climbing.about.com

Judging and Accepting Risk

The sport: white-water kayaking

How to start: find a kayaking group that can hook you up with training sessions and an easy class-1 or class-2 river

What to aim for: learn to research, navigate, and steer through class-3 or higher rapids

Think even bigger: a raucous trip on the Wenatchee River or Kicking Horse River, class-4 rapids that'll give you the ride of a lifetime

Resources:
www.americanwhitewater.org
www.gorp.away.com/gorp/activity/paddle.htm
www.beginnertriathlete.com

Asserting Your Individuality

The sport: snowboarding

How to start: get to the bottom of the hill with some skill and grace

What to aim for: drop into a half-pipe to learn how to grab and alley-oop

Think even bigger: off-trail riding, where you can rip and shred mightily and maybe even pull a few ollies

Resources:
www.snowboarding.com
www.abc-of-snowboarding.com
www.snowboarding.about.com

Leadership

The sport: adventure racing

How to start: train for a half- or full-day race

What to aim for: weekend-long Odyssey far from home, such as the Endorphin Fix in Canaan Valley, West Virginia

Think even bigger: try your luck at the Beast of the East race through the Adirondacks or the Canadian Death Race

Resources:
www.checkpointzero.com
www.usara.com
www.isportsdigest.tripod.com/adracing/main.html
www.oarevents.com/races.asp

Push way past your edge—and live to tell about it

Robyn Benincasa *takes on more adventure in one weeklong race than some people do in a lifetime. She's rappelled, climbed, kayaked, hiked, biked, and run under the most dire circumstances and in the farthest-flung locations you can imagine. It takes a lot—I mean a lot—to faze her.*

In Ecuador she fought altitude and oxygen-deprivation to scale a volcano. "I was drowning in air, crying, but I had to keep going for my team and for myself, so I wouldn't go home and be bummed for months." In Brazil her team got lost in the middle of the night, in a rainstorm, atop a mountain. "There was an insane downpour, thunder and lightning, mud everywhere, and our headlamps were out. I thought to myself, At least it's not Ecuador; at least I can breathe."

But even a pro like Benincasa has had a circumstance where her team decided that getting out of a situation safely was more important than holding on to their place in front of the pack. And she has a short list of risks she wishes she hadn't taken. "When you're sleep-deprived and your brain is fuzzy, it's hard to think well. And you don't have the reflexes you normally do," she says, which makes it tougher to both judge risk and manage risky situations adeptly.

Back to Brazil, again in the middle of the night: Her team came upon rapids that the rain had swelled from class-3 to class-4. "The organizers didn't halt the race. And it was near the end, so people were getting very competitive." The team in front of hers plunged ahead instead of waiting for daybreak, so her team felt compelled to do the same. "It was one of the stupidest things we've ever done. After the race, I thought, For what? What if someone had died?" she says. "You're always responsible for your own safety."

A word of caution:
How to avoid a major face-plant

1. Before plunging into an extreme training program or a strenuous vacation in a remote location, get a physical—even if you consider yourself to be in good shape.

2. Looks can be deceiving. Go easy at any new endeavor until you develop some judgment about your skill level and what is and isn't really tricky.

3. If you're serious about doing something well, get a coach.

173

4. Listen to people who know more than you do.

5. If your gut tells you that there's a good possibility you're about to get badly hurt, back off.

NEXT UP ▶
Extreme Rewards

Extreme Rewards

MODERATION IS A FATAL THING;
NOTHING SUCCEEDS LIKE EXCESS.

—Oscar Wilde

To say that an extreme career is its own reward probably sounds like a snow job. Work is work. You set goals and throw down your best performance because you expect to get something out of it.

No doubt, you expect a big part of what you get back to be in the form of cash. And, yeah, you should know what you're worth in the currency of your line of work—salary, bonus, stocks, options—and be willing to negotiate for it.

But it's not *all* about the money. If you think it is, you're missing the bigger picture of what you can get out of an extreme career.

An extreme career is a groove you get into that's self-perpetuating. Hard work creates opportunities, which allow you to perform at a higher level, which creates more opportunities. The rewards include having a say in when, how, and with whom you work, what types of projects you work on, and how work will fit into your life. It's doing all those things you want to do—and not doing things that bum you out—so you can make a ton of money *and* be proud about how you do it.

Consider...

Rick Alden and **Alain Chuard** and **Dave Alberga** finding ways to integrate the hobbies they love—snowboarding for Rick and Alain, cycling and triathloning for Dave—with the work they do.

Think of **Ben Wagner** weaving his awesome (and demanding) job at MTV, his avocation as a singer/songwriter, and his passion for running into one seamless life where each activity supports and feeds off of the others.

Remember how **Frank Karbe** convinced Goldman Sachs to hire him from a not-so-traditional background for investment banking. Then got the firm to let him sail around the world *and* sponsor his yacht. Then talked his bosses into moving him from Germany to San Francisco. And, finally, parted ways with Goldman when an awesome opportunity to do something new came his way.

Think of **Risa Shimoda** moving from M&M/Mars to Coca-Cola, and from New Jersey to Atlanta, to power up both her career and her kayaking skills.

> Hard work creates opportunities, which allow you to perform at a higher level, which creates more opportunities.

As Alberga points out, if you are performing at the level you should— seizing good opportunities and making the most of them—then the money stuff will happen, as it has for each of these folks. The other stuff—the quality of life and work stuff—is more important to strive for because it's harder to come by.

It's up to you to consider what else you really want out of work, above and beyond financial compensation.

Do you want...

the chance to work in London or Hong Kong or from home?

to be able to split your work time between a city office and a ski-country condo?

to have a dream team of colleagues or bosses whom you want to work with?

to be someone else's boss or just your own?

someone to give you money to start a business?

your big pay-off to be a year-end bonus—or your own IPO?

time off in chunks so you can travel the world or pursue a side passion?

to mix work and play or work and family? If not, how much time do you want to devote to each?

your boss to support, or your company to fund, a volunteer commitment that's important to you?

These kinds of opportunities are rewards to strive for and claim for yourself. They're the benefits you can reap from taking the plunge and committing to an extreme career path.

Each of the extreme careerists interviewed for this book has found a space, or a series of spaces, where they can earn a good living and be psyched to get up in the morning and go work toward whatever's next. That's the self-perpetuating groove that really *does* make an extreme career its own reward.

So, here's the strategy:

Whether your field is web design or copywriting or product development or biotech research or law or financial analysis, you go to work every day, and maybe to school, too, and you work on your skills.

Then you go out where people can see you and you rip, shred, and tear with style and confidence: You bring ideas to meetings, you develop proposals for your boss's boss, you volunteer to solo on a project or run a meeting, or to take charge of a situation that's psyching out everyone else.

And if you execute with awesome aggression and skill, you can create the opportunities you want, as well as awesome opportunities you didn't know you wanted. Layer these opportunities one on top of the other and you have an extreme career and its extreme rewards.

Where to start?

You start by setting awesome, impressive goals and saying to yourself, 'I want to grab *that* big air, and I think I can. But even if I can't, it's worth swallowing fear and accepting some risk, because along the way, I'll push my edge. I'll rip through cool embankments. I'll learn and accomplish things that I can't even imagine now. And I'm going to be psyched absolutely every day about what I'm doing and where it's taking me.

It beats the hell out of whining that your company hasn't laid out a clear career path for you, doesn't it?

177

SIGN & DATE

Resources

EXTREME ADVENTURES

Access Adventure Travel:
Learn to snowboard, surf, rock-climb, mountain-bike, or kayak on four-to-fifteen-day trips.
www.accesstrips.com

The Active Network:
Information on a range of action and extreme sports, including races and workshops around the country.
www.active.com

Adventure Society:
A range of activities for thrill-seekers in the New York area.
www.adventuresociety.com

Adventure Sports Online:
Lots of links for adventure and action-sports events and vacations.
www.adventuresportsonline.com

Adventure Travel Trade Association:
Links to adventure travel outfitters.
www.adventuretravel.biz

Appalachian Mountain Club:
Access to a wide range of outdoor activities in the northeast.
www.outdoors.org

Intrawest:
Well-planned helicopter skiing, hiking, and adventure trips for the deep-pocketed.
www.intrawest.com

Outward Bound:
They all but discovered the idea of finding your edge and pushing past it.
www.outwardbound.org

Thrill Planet:
Arranges skydiving, hang gliding, race-car driving, whitewater rafting, and rock climbing, among other adventures.
www.thrillplanet.com

United States Parachute Association:
Information on skydiving styles and schools around the U.S.
www.uspa.org

EXTREME READS

On the magazine rack...
Business Week: "And Now, the Chief Endurance Officer" (October 17, 2005).

Fast Company: "Extreme Jobs" (April 2005).

Fast Company: "Xtreme Teams" (November 1999).

Men's Journal: "Make Your Passion Pay" (October 2005).

Men's Journal: "Dream Jobs: The Best Jobs in America" (March 2005).

In the bookstore...
Ibarra, Herminia. *Working Identity: Unconventional Strategies for Reinventing Your Career* (Harvard Business School Press, 2003).

Lieber, Ron. *Upstart Start-ups!* (Broadway Books, 1998).

Nierenberg, Andrea R. *Nonstop Networking: How to Improve Your Life, Luck and Career* (Capital Books, 2002).

Shapiro, Eileen C. *Make Your Own Luck: 12 Practical Steps to Taking Smarter Risks in Business* (Portfolio, 2005).

Wademan, Daisy. *Remember Who You Are* (Harvard Business School Press, 2004)

Online...
www.careerjournal.com
www.ceochallenges.com
www.leadrenewal.com
www.mbaglobalnet.com
www.vault.com
www.worldclassteams.com

179

EXTREME SOURCES

Accenture. "Middle Manager Satisfaction Survey," October 2005.

www.benjaminwagner.com/journal

www.bls.gov (various studies by the Bureau of Labor Statistics).

Brown, Steven E.F. "Fastest Growing Companies." *San Francisco Business Times*, October 14, 2005.

DBM. "U.S. Career Transition Survey," July 2005.

www.elderweb.com

Family & Work Institute. "The National Study of the Changing Workforce," 2002.

International Labour Organization. "Job Stability in Industrialized Countries Remains Surprisingly Strong," www.ilo.org, 2003.

Morice, Laura. "Racing to the Extreme." *USA Today Weekend Magazine*, June 20, 2004.

Norcross, Don. "Iron Fans Endure, Too," *San Diego Union-Tribune*, October 17, 2005.

Peralta, Stacy. "Jay Adams: The Original." *Thrasher*, 1999.

Pfiffer, Jim. "Riding the Wind." *Elmira Star-Gazette*, August 28, 2005.

www.tonyhawk.com

Towers Perrin. "Employee Engagement Study," November 2005.

TripAdvisor. "Travel Trends Survey," November 2005.

Troughton, Jamie. "Emma Caught Between Rock, Hard Place," *Bay of Plenty Times*, October 19, 2005.

index

181

183

Acknowledgments

Special thank-yous to Sarah Scheffel at Quirk Packaging for bringing me this great opportunity to push *my* edge; to John and Stephanie Stislow of Stislow Design+Illustration for their ripping page designs and graphics, and Jill Alexander and Karen Cooper at Adams Media for their vision and extremely awesome support; to John Allen, Ted Kennedy, Neal Lenarsky, Ron Lieber, Andrea Nierenberg, Steve Mader, Rob Steir, and Rob Wyse for generously sharing their knowledge, Rolodexes, and much more, both for this book and over the years; to all the cool athletes and business people who carved time out of extremely full lives to talk to me; to my attorney, Anthony Elia; and, of course, to Richard Lang, with whom I rip, shred, and tear though the extreme adventure of life.